WE IN THE SHADOW

WE IN THE
SHADOW

**SURPRISING PLACES TO FIND HOPE
WHEN ALL APPEARS LOST AND GOD FAR AWAY.**

MICHAEL D. RILEY

WIPF & STOCK · Eugene, Oregon

WE IN THE SHADOW
Surprising Places to Find Hope When All Appears Lost and God Far Away

Wipf & Stock
An Imprint of Wipf and Stock Publishers
199 W. 8th Ave., Suite 3
Eugene, OR 97401

www.wipfandstock.com

PAPERBACK ISBN: 978-1-6667-6775-9
HARDCOVER ISBN: 978-1-6667-6776-6
EBOOK ISBN: 978-1-6667-6777-3

In Memory of . . .
Harold, Joanna, and Andrew

"This darkness and cloud is always between you and your God, no matter what you do, and it prevents you from seeing him clearly by the light of understanding in your reason and from experiencing him in sweetness of love in your affection."

– The Cloud of Unknowing,
Anonymous Author of the Late Fourteenth Century

CONTENTS

Acknowledgments

I am grateful for the congregations I served who became my conversational partners in the roller-coaster ride of life with God. Many of these people became my soulmates as we awkwardly wrestled with the challenges of faith and the mysterious and elusive presence of God. When the journey grew murky and we stumbled along the way, we found strength in one another and discovered God's presence closer than we imagined and in places we often overlooked. When my life reaches its end and I have finished my course and, hopefully, kept the faith, it will only be because these people stood with me through thick and thin.

I am indebted to pastors Timothy Moody, Paul Wrenn, Ron Rowe, Jim Chavis, Bob Burroughs, and George Mason who took precious time away from their busy schedules to read early drafts and make constructive critiques. Chaplain Ed Wilder, who has spent much of his life caring for sick and suffering people, was an important resource. Professors Thomas Long and Dixon Sutherland contributed important criticisms that made the book better. Thanks to Tim Broderick for pushing me to make the book available to a wider audience and for designing the front cover and for seeing the book through to publication. A special thanks to my go-to-guy for computer problems Nitin Athavale, whose skill in exorcising technical gremlins kept me somewhat sane. Heartfelt appreciation goes to longtime friends Bobbie and Charles Cottle, Melvonna Schneider, Kirk Landau, Doug Roseborough, and Cecil Wells for reading the book and helping me to think and write for people both within and outside the church.

Without the editing skills and encouragement of Julia Roller, the book never would have crossed the finish line. Writing a book is not just a solitary endeavor but requires collaboration with others. I worked with Julia throughout the writing process and her guidance has been indispensable. I always looked forward to her edits, and even when they weren't flattering, they were always sensitive and kind. Thank you, Julia. I take full responsibility, however, for any errors that remain within the book.

Most of all I am thankful for my wife who read draft after draft with patience and made invaluable and insightful suggestions. The spouse of a minister lives an emotionally draining life, filled with a wide array of daily challenges. I am forever grateful to be married to a person who met the burdensome days and sleepless nights with grace. She adds immeasurable joy to my life. Thank you DeDe for sharing your life with me.

Preface

People of faith generally fall into one of two categories. People in the first category confidently claim to have a personal relationship with God/Jesus, while people in the second category yearn for God but struggle with what constitutes a personal relationship with God or wonder if a personal relationship with God is even possible. Most Christians, especially of the evangelical persuasion, fall into the first category. *We in the Shadow* has been written for those in the second group.

The belief that God is personally engaged in our individual lives has comforted millions of people through the centuries, but today that belief is under enormous stress. The randomness of violence, suffering, and inexplicable evil has pushed believers to question the reliability and personal nature of God. How can we encounter divine presence when so often God appears deaf to our prayers and indifferent to our pain? Unless this question can somehow be practically and thoughtfully answered, faith will be viewed as an option only for those who skim over the incomprehensibly cruel surfaces of life with eyes closed and fingers stuck firmly in their ears.

We in the Shadow reflects almost forty years of caring for people in pastoral ministry, listening to their faith stories and trying to relate Scripture to them in light of those stories. Over the course of my ministry I spent significant time with people who had given up on God. They had been led to believe that God was personally and directly involved in their lives but when faced with a crisis, God seemed either to disappear or turn his back on their collapsing world. These people for the most part did not become traditional atheists, philosophically opposed to theism, but simply lost confidence in the God they had once trusted. They moved on with their lives, maybe not formally divorced from God but certainly separated, living in a kind of melancholy shadow of faith.

Their spiritual disillusionment troubled me, especially when I looked into their faces and saw eyes filled with despair, empty of hope. How could I as their pastor help them understand that maybe their image of God was only a partial picture of faith? How could I gently share with people who were dear to me that perhaps their expectations of God were based more on popular traditions than biblical stories of faith? Could I help people struggling through the wintry season grasp that God's presence may not be so very far away, if only they knew where to look?

We in the Shadow is my pastoral response. It is my way of reaching out to untold numbers of people who struggle with faith in a personal God or who have lost hope in a God who matters. Perhaps you have wandered away from the community of faith because God seems either to be absent or disinterested in your broken world. Maybe you feel ill at ease in a church culture that views negative or apathetic feelings toward God with suspicion or even hostility. Or you might be one of countless people in today's world who has lost faith in God completely, yet feels a spiritual emptiness within.

If so, it is my prayer that *We in the Shadow* can lead you to discover a more spiritually authentic understanding of how God can be present in your life. It is my belief that God's personal nature can be experienced, just not in the culturally popular way we have been led to believe. God does matter, and when God is present with us, there is hope.

There are many excellent English translations of the Bible available today. I have chosen The New Revised Standard Version (NRSV) as my primary translation. On occasion, however, I also used The New International Version (NIV). Where the biblical texts are marked by an endnote, the translation is my own.

A CHRISTMAS EVE STORY

Always, they tell you to go where God calls you.
What they don't say is that,
sometimes God will call you to the wilderness,
gesture toward the trees,
and then hang back and wave you on alone.

- Molly McCully Brown
Poet with Cerebral Palsy

The highlight of the year for many churches is the Christmas Eve service. While Easter may be more theologically significant, the enthusiasm
for Christmas by both young and old is unmatched. Even though as a pastor
I participated in close to forty of these Yuletide celebrations, one particular Christmas Eve stands out in my memory. The night began like so many
others with my family and me driving to the church in anticipation of the
seasonal event. The car was rocking with playful banter as my wife and
two sons rather impiously rehearsed their parts for the lighting of the final
candle of the Advent season, the Christ Candle, the candle that represents
God's presence in the world. Our boys good-naturedly traded barbs as they
recited their lines, teasing each other when one failed to remember a word or

1

garbled the pronunciation. The holiday mood has a way of laying to rest even sibling rivalry.

For much of the world Christmas is a festive time. The cheerful music, parties, days off from work, gifts from loved ones and friends, and delicious treats make for a change of pace from the daily stresses of life. Christmas provides a needed respite from the often harsh and unrelenting realities of everyday existence.

This Christmas Eve was different, at least for me. I was not thinking of Advent or anything related to this joyous season of the year. My thoughts were far away. A few hours earlier I had finished reading Elie Wiesel's *Night*. It is a short book but certainly not a quick read. For the previous two or three days I had lingered over one passage after another, not able emotionally to absorb what Wiesel had written. A Stephen King novel pales in comparison to the horrors of Wiesel's *Night*. Wiesel's story was no imaginative nightmare; it was unimaginable reality.

After I squeezed my car between a SUV and a pick-up truck, I tried to re-direct my attention to the Advent celebration. I, too, had a speaking role and mentally tried to rehearse my few lines, but my concentration just wasn't there. My mind drifted back to Wiesel's incomprehensible story of terror, imagining men, women, and children gasping for breath as poison pellets dropped from the air vents above the boarded-up and locked shower room at Auschwitz, Nazi Germany's most notorious death camp. I tried to block images of trembling and naked bodies pressing ever more closely together, desperately trying to find space away from the poisonous gas, but I could not rid my mind of the vision. I became slightly nauseous as I conjured up the shrill sounds of terrified screams and pleading prayers.

Elie was only a fifteen-year-old teenager when he and his family were transported to the infamous Auschwitz extermination camp in occupied Poland. The evening they arrived a tall chimney was shooting out flames and emitting heavy smoke. Elie smelled "an abominable odor floating through the air," an odor he would later realize was charred human flesh.[1] When the young teen stepped off the train, he could see the abject fear on people's faces and sense the evil that hung like a toxic mist over the camp, suffocating any remnant of hope.

He writes, "Never shall I forget the little faces of the children, whose bodies I saw turned into wreaths of smoke beneath a silent blue sky. Never shall I forget those flames which consumed my faith forever."[2] The poignant sentences reverberated throughout my being, setting my heart on edge. It was as if the whole world had collapsed into a ghastly pyre of little children.

2

Faith in a benevolent and attentive God, like the cremated bodies, melted into ash that night for Elie Wiesel. To see loved ones, friends, and neighbors murdered simply because they were Jews snuffed out the spiritual flame that had once burned so brightly in his no-longer-innocent heart. He would spend the remainder of his life trying to make some sense out of that madness.

As a child Elie had been sensitive to the presence of God, had studied the Talmud and longed to read the mystic writings of the cabbala. The driving passion in his life was to serve God but that night in Auschwitz, having witnessed unimaginable slaughter, Elie Wiesel "had become a completely different person. The student of the Talmud. . . . had been consumed in the flames. There remained only a shape that looked like me. A dark flame had entered into my soul and devoured it."[3]

Going to church with my family on Christmas Eve, I could not shake the disturbing scene Elie Wiesel had described. I had read a number of books on the Holocaust, but *Night* captivated me with its intimate eye-witness detail offered by a fifteen-year-old boy in a way no other book had. When I listened to the backseat laughter of our two boys, one of whom had just turned fifteen, it unnerved me to think of them suffering through such a hellish nightmare.

Yet, one million boys and girls, not to mention five million men and women, were brutally murdered in the death camps. What Elie Wiesel and so many other people endured is unfathomable. How could any person of faith not be affected by such meaningless human savagery? Faith in a compassionate and personal God would forever be on trial, not just for Jews but for all people of faith. I felt no condemnation for Elie Wiesel's renunciation of faith that night, only understanding and sympathy.

With the engine finally turned off our boys bolted out of the car and we hurried toward the sanctuary. The parking lot was almost full and seemed alive with laughter and Christmas greetings as moms, dads, and children excitedly slammed car doors and made their way toward the Christmas Eve service. As we entered the sanctuary, I could see that the festive crowd would be large. Already the cavernous room was nearing capacity. Ushers were bringing in extra chairs to accommodate the holiday overflow. Christmas carols were softly being piped into the auditorium through the speaker system.

People greeted me with "Merry Christmas, Pastor!" I walked down the church aisles seeing smiles and happy faces all around. I had always enjoyed the Christmas season. Everything is a bit lighter, people appear more tolerant, daily tensions fade from memory, at least for a few days.

I tried to hide my heaviness of heart; I smiled, shook hands with parents and asked little children if they were ready for Christmas. From time to time I looked around the room and wondered if there were other people here who were also hiding behind masks of smiles, whose hearts were heavy with worry or grief or pain.

I spotted a young mom in her early thirties who was battling breast cancer. For several years she had courageously fought the relentless disease, but her pallid face and sunken cheeks warned of more difficult days ahead. I knew she worried little about herself, but who would care for her small child? Would her pre-school daughter remember Mommy? She smiled at me, but I thought I could see behind her mask. Her eyes betrayed anxiety and fear.

In the pew across the aisle from me sat an elderly man whose wife had died of a lung disease a few years earlier. I tried to catch his attention, but he stared blankly out into the throng of people milling about. He was losing his eyesight and would soon live in darkness. His face was serene, as though he had made peace with his fate. Had he? I wondered.

A tall, slender man, about my age, made his way toward me. Only a few months earlier his wife had been killed on her way to church by a speeding truck that had run a red light. His face was empty of expression. He put his hand on my shoulder but said nothing. His two pre-teen sons stood silently beside him. There were no words that could assuage their sorrow. Their pool of grief was too deep. For a few quiet seconds we wrapped our arms around each other, then the father pulled back and after a moment said to me, "It just doesn't feel like Christmas." Was he reading my mind? Was he, too, hiding behind a mask?

As I scanned the congregation, I suspected there were other people here who found it difficult to imbibe the holiday spirit, people laboring under the heavy burden of life. Much of the world is a tragic place, a place of loneliness and grief, suffering and pain, sickness and death. In the modern world we have become adept at camouflaging the misery and ugliness of existence. But just behind a thin veil of manufactured illusion, human inequities, gross injustices, and unimaginable suffering are readily noticeable.

Still, I am grateful for the Christmas season. Christmas has a way of blurring our vision by thickening that veil for a few blissful days, allowing us a brief escape from the world's brutal realities, the way a fresh layer of winter snow covers the dead grass and overgrown flower beds.

As the service started I made my way to my seat and listened pensively as the choir sang Joy to the World. A few moments later my family dutifully lit the Christ Candle—the candle promising the hope of God's presence. With all the Advent candles softly glowing the congregation joined in with the choir and sang a couple of Christmas carols, and then I gave a brief homily.

The end of the service was marked with each person holding a lighted candle and singing Silent Night. The muted flames flickering in the darkened sanctuary reflected tender warmth on contented and excited faces. How near and intimate God's presence. How easy it was to believe in God's goodness and love. As I scanned the congregation, my mind was still filled with the image of a fifteen-year-old boy silently watching human ash raining gently down over Auschwitz.

CHAPTER 1

I WANT ANSWERS.
TO DATE, NOTHING.

The fundamental problem of human existence,
the question of God's trustworthiness,
constitutes the single most significant theological issue of today.

- James Crenshaw

As far back as I can remember I have been fascinated by the night sky. Lying on my back in our yard as a child, I would spend hours mesmerized by the starry heavens, trying to form animal outlines by connecting the tiny dots of flickering lights. Our babysitter explained to my older brother and me that the stars were windows from which God and the angels could look down from heaven and see us and protect us from any harm. Even now in my eighth decade I remember how comforting that thought was to a four-year-old boy.

My parents were not particularly religious, but they were insistent that my brother and I attend Sunday School on a regular basis. It was in Mr. Carpenter's fifth grade class where I learned that God knew my name and even had the hairs of my head numbered. God is so attentive to creation, Mr. Carpenter shared with the class, that not even a bird falls from its nest unnoticed. There is no place on earth, he assured us, where God's presence does not dwell. These early religious teachings left me feeling perfectly secure in a world where God and the angels stood sentinel, ready to fend off any evils that might come my way.

But those warm feelings didn't last. Life happened. And slowly my childhood theology gave way to a much more disturbing and less predictable world, a world where children are not always protected and God can sometimes appear inattentive or even worse, indifferent. The change of course didn't occur all at once, but day after day I grew to realize that the simple faith I was taught as a child was anything but simple. Life is just too unpredictable and cruel, and it didn't take me long to see some of life's tragedies up-close. A high school friend's suicide triggered questions that caused me to second-guess God's providential care. Only a few days before we had been unruly teenagers sitting side by side in an Algebra class. Were God and the angels somehow distracted while my friend's troubles overwhelmed him? Shortly afterwards my forty-seven-year-old father had a massive stroke, severely crippling him, and his death a few years later further rattled my now shaky theology. While a sophomore in college I heard on the radio of a chartered airplane full of college football players that had crashed in a storm, killing everyone on board. Later, I learned that I had played against many of those victims in high school, and their tragic deaths continued to erode the innocence of my childhood faith.

Tragedies and other horrific events have a way of unraveling the threads of our childhood beliefs. While some people may decide to turn away from faith in God altogether, others may choose to deconstruct their childhood faith and examine the remnants to see if enough threads remain to stitch together a more authentic way to believe in a God who is personal and attentive.

My childhood babysitter and Sunday School teacher may not have been wrong to believe that God watches over us, but maybe they misunderstood how God watches over us. If we selectively pull out a few biblical verses here and there to support our view of how we think the universe should operate, we may temporarily find comfort, but we will also set ourselves up for eventual heartbreak. Sooner or later life will punch us in the nose, and we won't be able to stop the bleeding.

The belief in a God who is personally and directly attentive to each individual life can be seductive, but when overwhelmed by life's cruel realities, we may develop a more hardened view of the world that no longer leaves room for God. Tragedy and unrelenting suffering have a way of robbing us of any sense of God's presence. In such extreme times we may give in to despair and turn away from faith. After all, if God cannot be counted on when our backs are up against the wall, then why even bother?

But what if there is a larger story of faith, a story that has too often been muddled by the modern world, a story that reveals God's nearness, just not in the way we have been traditionally led to believe? What if God is actually closer than we think? What if we have misinterpreted how God watches over us and how God is with us? And what if, by not having a more complete story, we have grown unfairly disillusioned with God?

In my almost forty years of serving as a pastor to several different congregations the question, "Is God directly and personally involved in our lives?" was put to me more times than I can remember. People asked the question in a variety of ways but the intent was the same: Can we count on God to be with us when the going gets tough? The random nature of evil, indiscriminately attacking its victims without regard to any rational standard, gives off mixed signals regarding God's personal involvement, leaving people confused and uncertain as to God's dependability. To be able to count on God's presence in times of adversity is of fundamental importance to people of faith and without that assurance people will grow weary and lose confidence in God. For those who believe in God this question stands above all others.

WHEN LIFE HAPPENS

As a pastor I saw my share of life's cruel and often inexplicable tragedies. Church members involved in a gruesome accident, the sudden unexpected death of a young person in her prime or a bleak medical prognosis for a new born infant were frequent interruptions to my daily schedule. A pastor friend of mine once told me that interruptions were his work, and any pastor who takes ministry seriously would agree. I tried not to let the unpredictable intrusions of these all-too-frequent events callus me to heartache and sorrow. People struggling through grief and pain desperately need someone to share their burden, someone who cares, someone to be with them.

The twentieth-century preacher A. J. Gossip once said, "You people in the sunshine may believe the faith, but we in the shadow must believe it. We have nothing else."[1] Tragedy can and does turn its hapless victims toward faith in God. History is replete with stories of famous personalities who found faith during troubled times. Abraham, Moses, the Apostle Paul, Augustine, Luther, and a host of others moved toward God during upheavals in their lives. Dark times can stir the heart to seek a spiritual power beyond this world.

The opposite can also be true. Sometimes the harrowing experiences of life can destroy our confidence and trust in God. Many of the Jews who survived the Nazi death camps turned their backs on God or reconstructed a different way of understanding their religion. Richard Rubenstein's *After Auschwitz* vividly recounts how after the extermination of six million Jews, a million of them children, faith lost its innocence for many. Absurd and gratuitous suffering can and does harden hearts against God.

Life is challenging and made more daunting by senseless tragedy. Some misfortune, of course, we bring upon ourselves. If I smoke for thirty years and develop heart and lung disease, I rolled the dice and lost. I have no one to blame but myself. It is true that some people throw caution to the wind and seemingly escape the consequences of their self-destructive behavior. While we may wonder why some people seemingly get off easy, we shake our heads in quiet resignation at those who gambled and lost. Rationally, we understand that most people, sooner or later, tend to pay when playing a game of chance.

And then, of course, there is the pain that we inflict on each other. In our modern world we read of mass shootings, terrorist bombings, and all kinds of other inhumane acts we bring upon ourselves. I wonder sometimes if humankind doesn't have a death wish.

Of course, not all forms of pain and suffering are evil. When we touch a hot stove, for instance, the pain is intense, but from that experience we grow and learn about the world. Much of the pain that we incur from day-to-day living helps us to navigate through life. Some suffering can and does make us stronger, wiser, and more sensitive. But there is a limit. When pain and suffering serve no purpose other than the destruction of its victim, then it becomes a tool of evil.

It is this destructive, evil suffering that troubles me, whether created by us or some malevolent force. Distinguishing on philosophical or theological grounds the categories of evil and suffering may be intellectually satisfying and can be helpful to a point, but to those caught in the web of evil, these distinctions are meaningless. As a rule, regardless of cause, most people suffer far more than they deserve. We are more victims than sinners.

What disturbs me most deeply, what creates tension with my childhood faith and pushes me to doubt the providential design of the universe, is when we play by the rules and still lose. Unexplained or innocent suffering threatens, some would even say obliterates, the belief that God watches over us and is personally engaged in our lives.

A few years ago my wife and I spent the morning of January third in an oncologist's reception room. One of our closest friends had an appointment with the doctor, and we wanted to be there for him when he came out of the conference room. In mid-December his family doctor had recommended that he see a specialist because of a lingering cough. The specialist ordered a battery of tests to determine the nature of a suspicious-looking shadow on his lungs. As a result Steve's Christmas had been filled with anxiety and mood swings. He was only fifty-nine-years-old and had lived a healthy lifestyle, but the doctor had warned that his condition could be serious.

When the door to the doctor's office opened and Steve and his wife walked out, one look at their faces told us the news had not been good. Steve's typically placid countenance revealed tell-tale signs of anxiety. His eyes were locked in focused thought as he walked slowly toward us. He sat down in a chair next to mine and his face broke into a sort of half-crooked grin, more forced than natural. He said rather matter-of-factly, "Well, it's cancer." Striving for nonchalance, he and his wife tried to reassure us that everything would be fine, and we didn't need to worry, but I was not convinced. Sometimes people of faith feel the need to hide their fear and anxiety in dire circumstances and project a happy face as a sign of trust in God.

Steve explained to us that the diagnosis was Stage IV Renal Cell Carcinoma, a virulent form of kidney cancer. Later, over a cup of coffee, Steve spoke as though he were reciting a poem in a high school English class of treatment options and possible future surgeries to remove the affected kidney. As I studied his face, I sensed he was struggling to stay composed and was simply parroting what he had heard from the oncologist. Only a month or so earlier he had believed he was in excellent health, but now he was fighting for his life.

In the days that followed I spoke with Steve by phone and left a few text messages. I wanted him to know that if he needed me, I would be there for him.

Not many days afterwards Steve showed up at my office. He tried to make himself comfortable in a chair opposite mine but fidgeted for several moments as though he was uncertain whether he wanted to stay. I began by asking him how he was holding up.

Slowly the words spilled out. The diagnosis had caught him off guard. "I didn't think my life would end this way," he said. As he spoke of his wife and two sons, his voice was flat. He showed no emotion. It was as though the life had already drained out of him. He told me he thought he would die sooner than later. "I'm not sure what to do. . ." his voice trailed off. "There is nothing in my life that has prepared me for what I'm facing." His pale face betrayed the anxiety and despair I had seen so often in the faces of terminally ill patients in hospice centers. He had dark circles under his eyes, and he appeared tired, completely listless, as though the cancer had swallowed up every cell of energy.

In the weeks that followed Steve began writing a blog to chronicle his journey of life with cancer. In one of his earlier blogs Steve expressed his frustration over the uncertainty that now shadowed his life:

> *Emotionally, it's been a roller coaster and I hate roller coasters.*
> *I want solid answers, I want to know if this drug is going to work,*
> *I want to know what is in store down the road.*
> *I want God to stand beside me and tell me what he has in*
> *store for me. I want answers. To date, nothing.*

His topsy-turvy world continued to rise and fall during the next few weeks. There were days when the medical reports gave Steve hope and his spirits would soar, but there were also days of discouraging lows. He lost weight and his face took on an ashen look, and I sensed Steve knew he was losing the battle.

One Sunday after church he and his wife took my wife and me out to lunch. Over a bowl of pasta he talked of his love for the Kentucky Wildcats basketball team, his enjoyment of kayaking and, naturally, his family. He told me that he had not lost his faith in God, but he questioned where God was. "Sometimes, I feel as though God has forgotten me. I pray, 'Okay, God, it's me, Steve, remember me? I could use a little help here!' And then nothing. It is as if he has misplaced my address." He looked at me for a long moment, hoping, perhaps, I would say something that might lift the fog that had blanketed his life.

I wanted to ease my friend's anxiety but the thoughts dancing around in my head seemed superficial and inane. I knew passages in Scripture that promised God's presence and protection in times of trouble, but he knew those verses too. Besides, quoting a verse or two of Scripture to someone who is staring death in the face, if not carefully and wisely constructed, can ring somewhat hollow. When I finally did respond and attempt a few words of comfort, Steve shifted the conversation to another topic.

Just three months after his diagnosis his wife called me early one Saturday morning just after midnight. "Michael, he's gone. Steve's gone!" My wife and I hurriedly dressed and drove to the emergency room where we found Steve's lifeless body lying on a table in an examining room. Unexpectedly, his lungs had filled with fluid and in spite of efforts to revive him, his heart had just stopped beating. The roller coaster had come to an abrupt end.

Although I have witnessed numerous deaths and presided over countless funerals in my forty years of pastoral ministry, Steve's death touched me in a way no other loss had. I had buried close friends before, even mourned the passing of both of my parents and my brother, but their deaths, while filled with sorrow and pain, had not affected me to the extent that my friend's had.

I continue to be haunted by what Steve wrote in his blog: "I want God to stand beside me and tell me what he has in store for me." When Steve stumbled through the most difficult journey of his life, he didn't experience the intimacy and closeness with God he longed for and had expected. God felt distant, as though God had indeed lost his address. My friend could not understand why God had seemingly abandoned him in his desperate hour of need.

WHEN LIFE FALLS APART

When life unexpectedly takes a turn and suddenly everything falls apart, few people know how to respond, as most of us have little practice with sudden, unanticipated calamities. We don't spend time preparing for a cancer diagnosis or a tragic accident or some other unforeseen event. Those things just happen and when they do, they catch us off guard. Religiously bent people are told that a strong faith is our best preparation, and by building a solid spiritual foundation, when the winds blow and the storms rage, God will be there with us and our faith will see us through. But what happens when during a time of crisis God doesn't show up and our faith foundation cracks?

As a pastor I have observed that even the most formidable faith may buckle, and no one is immune to the effects of feeling abandoned by God. Feelings of doubt, despair, and depression can jar the faith of even the most dedicated believer and when the storms of life attack us, we often discover to our dismay that faithful obedience does not necessarily protect us or grant us privileged accessibility to God. And when feeling vulnerable and alone, even the most robust faith may collapse.

How do we cope when the door is slammed in our faces on our supposed personal relationship with God and we no longer sense divine presence? Unrelenting pain has a way of eroding the most zealous of faiths. When we wake every day to more suffering, either mental or physical, with no relief on the horizon, who among us can stand up to that? Our prayers go unanswered, spiritual resources dry up and God's presence fades into a distant memory. We, too, want answers.

We are often told by well-meaning church leaders that the men and women of the biblical era endured every trial and tribulation without wavering in their faith. To doubt or to curse our circumstances betrays a flaw in character, maybe even reveals a lack of faith. Consequently, when we have been battered by life's tragedies, we may suppress our feelings of having been forsaken by God, leaving us with feelings of anger, guilt, and confusion.

Our sense of shame may be compounded by the response of our faith community. Unaccustomed to hearing complaints directed against God, the faith community may discourage us from sharing our raw feelings of anguish and spiritual emptiness. We grieve now not only from a particular trage-dy confronting us—a shattered life, the unexpected death of a loved one, a nightmarish disease or a freakish accident—but also the denied opportunity to tell our faith story simply because it may not align with the traditionally accepted beliefs.

My friend Steve recounted some of his emotions and thoughts in his blog, but he confessed to me on several occasions that he dare not write the most disturbing questions that filled his mind for fear that some of those feelings would have been too X-rated for his church friends to digest. So they remained buried deeply within him where they caused additional unrest. He worried that there might be something seriously wrong within his own heart. Why did he feel so alone? Why did he have so much anger? Why did he feel as though God had lost his address? Why did he feel so hopeless? Had the opportunity been presented to him to share these feelings with a sympathet-ic community, perhaps these troubling questions would have been addressed as natural faith responses instead of signs of a spiritual foundation in need of repair. Maybe the faith community could have absorbed some of Steve's emotional and spiritual trauma and provided a spiritual catharsis, releasing him from his guilt and shame.

It is unfortunate that some faith communities consider talk about the cold and barren days of faith as a spiritual weakness or an act of willful disobedience. An authentic and vibrant faith, we are sometimes told, has the strength to push past these disquieting emotions. We may be encouraged to meditate on God's goodness and love, to pray without ceasing, and, if we do, we are promised that our anxiety and feelings of divine betrayal will pass. Unfortunately, for many people their sense of loneliness and rejection doesn't recede but only deepens to the point where they feel jilted by God, marooned in an indifferent universe, a universe without meaning, without hope. That spiritual void soon crushes any previous confidence or trust in divine providence. Yes, they can play the pretend game that everything is fine, and they can learn to say all the right things, but to bury their pain and grief does not make it less real. Their deep-seated feelings of divine abandonment may lie dormant within them, but sooner or later those dark emotions will awaken and create an even greater sense of hopelessness.

As difficult as it is for some of us to acknowledge, life with God is not all sunshine. There exists a shadow side to faith, a region where God seems distant and far away, where clouds of doubt and disillusionment obscure any path toward hope. There are many people who feel imprisoned in this darker region, and, unfortunately, they may find possible escape blocked by their own faith community.

The faith community often finds it difficult to take seriously and empathize with this darker side of life with God. Much of the church culture embraces an optimistic and feel-good faith as the only acceptable model. Some churches feel threatened by those who live in the shadow of belief, who question the goodness and compassion of God. Churches are often guilty of having selective memories, focusing only on the beautiful and joyous portraits of faith. Have we forgotten that Jesus was "a man of sorrows, and acquainted with grief" (Isa. 53:3)? Have we been in such a rush to celebrate Easter that we have skipped over Good Friday and overlooked the grizzly scene of a man being crucified?

Yes, there is much joy in Christian faith, but there is also heartache and sorrow. To affirm the rosier side of faith without acknowledging the darker side leaves those of us whose eyes have grown dim with grief without support, especially the strength that comes from an understanding faith community.

How wonderful it would be if the church invited and welcomed spiritually distressed and troubled people to share their faith journeys and comforted them in their spiritual struggles. When we find ourselves confused, frightened, and uncertain about our relationship with God, when the light of faith burns dimly or not at all, we can quickly lose hope and without hope, darkness will overwhelm us. I have come to believe that the community of faith can be a refuge for those in the shadow, for those mired in the space between belief and unbelief, and by serving as an amorphous place for hope, the faith community may open a pathway to God.

In the following pages we will see that even the celebrated heroes of biblical times, on occasion, grappled with affirming God as benevolent, caring, and attentive. In other words, people like Abraham, Moses, Jeremiah, the disciples, and so many others rode a similar roller-coaster of faith that we in the modern world do. According to the biblical witness, anger, doubt, complaint, and even cursing were characteristics of their faith journeys and not necessarily signs of unbelief.

These more melancholic faith stories occupy a surprisingly large space in the Bible. People who felt abandoned or rejected by God are given ample voice in the pages of Scripture, and neither the Old Testament nor the New shy away from sharing faith stories that bordered on despair or hung on by a thread to belief in a loving God. Instead of chastising these tortured believers, the Bible canonized their spiritual journeys as witnesses to what it means to be a person of faith. Instead of ignoring these voices the modern church would profit by listening closely to what these people have to say.

When my friend, Steve, looked to me to say something hopeful, I will forever regret that I did not point him to people in the Bible who also wanted answers, who also prayed that God would stand beside them but who so often felt alone. These people desperately hoped to discover some trace of God in the midst of their collapsing world but often felt only frustration and abandonment. Haven't we all been there at one time or another?

Unfortunately, I can no longer speak with my friend. But there are others, like him, who no doubt are saying, "I want answers, God. Why are you so far from me? Why can't you come and stand beside me? Where can I find some flicker of hope in these unending days of darkness?"

Perhaps you are one of them. If so, this book is for you.

CHAPTER 2

SPINES ARE NOT MADE OF STEEL

We both believe and disbelieve
a hundred times an Hour,
which keeps Believing nimble.

- Emily Dickinson

As I squirmed and tried to get comfortable on a cold examining table, the medical technician repeated, "Please lie perfectly still, Mr. Riley." His words struck me as crass, even inhumane. From the moment the attendant wheeled me into the radiology room I had felt nothing but embarrassment and humiliation. The bright lights and the sterile environment offered no comfort or warmth. I was told to remove my hospital gown and then climb onto a table and lie still, completely naked. As I lay exposed, the technicians spread my legs and arms and began drawing lines on my body with some kind of marker. Three days earlier an exploratory surgery had found an aggressive malignancy in my lower intestinal area. Now the doctors were trying to assess whether the cancer had spread to other parts of my body before they operated to remove seventy-five to eighty lymph nodes along my spine.

The technicians chatted casually with each other as they worked. One of them, a young woman just a few years younger than I, giggled at one of her partner's comments as she raised my arm to make another mark. I wondered if this was what a lab specimen felt like under a microscope. It was almost as if I were already a cadaver, a mere corpse without feelings or emotions.

I was a thirty-three-year-old pastor with a wife and two small children. In my early twenties I had made a decision to enter the ministry. Even though my family was not a particularly religious one, life with God intrigued me. I had read the Bible through several times by the time I entered college, and prayed throughout the day, and tried to live a moral and ethical life. I believed that God was personal and involved in the minutest details of my life.

In college I played football, even managing to letter. I had been healthy and took pride in keeping my body fit, but now I was a cancer patient with an uncertain prognosis. The kind of cancer that had grown inside of me claimed the lives of more than half of its victims within five years.

Lying helplessly on the table, listening to the staff discuss their personal lives, I felt incredibly insignificant. For the first time in my life the possibility of death washed over me, leaving in its wake feelings of loneliness and despair. Focusing on the ceiling I blinked furiously, fighting to keep the pool of water collecting in my eyes from running down my cheeks.

During more carefree times, God's presence had seldom been an issue. When blessing followed blessing, I had little reason to question the faithfulness of God, but in the few days since I'd received the verdict of a possible death sentence, when I desperately needed some sign from God, some sense of divine presence, there was only silence. I now felt fragile, empty, alone, so alone—just a diseased body in a radiology room lying on a metal slab. The only sounds were the voices of those making colored drawings on my anatomy and the periodic humming of the machine mapping my exposed flesh. Staring into the light I felt only darkness.

DISTURBING QUESTIONS

Life can be incredibly harsh. There is nothing fair about it, and among those of us who believe in God and believe that God is personal and caring, life's unfairness can cause a major crisis of faith. We can absorb only so much before we surrender to hopelessness. Within wide segments of the faith community there is belief that God is in control, that whatever happens has been ordained, directed or allowed by God. We are taught that not even a bird falls from its nest without God's knowledge or tacit approval. The structure of the universe adheres to God's plan where the wicked receive their just desserts while the righteous prosper in all they do. Biblical chapters and verses are cited as proof texts to affirm that those who honor God will be rewarded in this life, but those who do evil will meet with disaster now and in the world to come.

The idea that God loves us and somehow watches over our welfare has become a bedrock conviction. An uncaring and distant God would have little relevance. Only a God who interacts with us, who is involved in our daily struggles, is worthy of worship and praise.

But how does God watch over us? Does God work directly on our behalf to deflect the evils that come our way? Is God personally attuned to our every need? Does God engage with us on a personal and intimate level?

Much of traditional church teaching answers, "Yes," and this time-honored way of understanding how God operates in the world has wound itself tightly around the core belief system within the faith community. It offers assurance and comfort and provides a worldview that stabilizes life, particularly in tumultuous times. But how are we affected when that traditional understanding breaks down? What happens when we are confronted with tragedy or our innocent child is diagnosed with a terminal disease or is born with severe disabilities? What happens to our faith in a personal God when day after day we feel that God has forgotten us? How do we speak of God's love when a natural disaster wipes out tens of thousands of people?

These questions are not abstract theological "what ifs." Too many times in my ministry I have sat with grieving parents or teens or children who struggled to make sense out of similarly inexplicable tragedies. After the 2004 tsunami in Indonesia killed more than 200,000 people, a teenager asked me after a church service, "Pastor, do you think anyone believes in God anymore?" She was not fishing for an argument from her pastor. She had seen graphic images on television of death and destruction and her confidence in the God she had been taught to believe in was badly shaken, maybe even shattered.

During my years as a pastor I spent considerable time caring for people whose trust in God had seemingly been betrayed. Sickness, loss of job, broken marriage, death, and an assortment of other woes created fissures of doubt as to whether God was dependable. In all fairness the bulk of my duties centered on happy times—a promotion at work, the birth of a child, the marriage of two people. When death did occur, more often than not it involved an elderly person and in these circumstances death, while not without grief, was usually a blessing, not a tragedy. That is why the traditional understanding of God as personal and benevolent works so well—life, at least for those of us in advanced countries, runs fairly smoothly most of the time.

Except, of course, when it doesn't. There is another side to life, one that begs to be explored, and one that raises serious questions about the personal nature of God. While there is much good in the world, there is also much evil, and sometimes that evil throws a monkey wrench into the gears of a well-ordered universe where God supposedly has built a hedge of protection around those who are faithful. Too often I have been present by the bedside of children, teenagers and young adults whose fractured and diseased bodies are evidence that sometimes that supposed wall collapses. Even old age is no guarantee of a peaceful exit from this world. Many of us have been devastated when our aged parents no longer could recognize us or remember our names.

There is much injustice and cruelty in our world and sooner or later almost all of us become victims. To knowingly turn our backs on this brutal truth and ignore its effects leaves faith in an attentive and personal God an option only for the lucky few who have somehow managed to postpone the harsh realities of existence.

THE QUESTION OF GOD'S PERSONAL NATURE

If we believe in a God who is personal and loving, then events like natural disasters, birth defects, disease, inexplicable failures of our bodies to work properly and a host of other misfortunes challenge this concept. A case can be made that this particular understanding of God has somehow failed to tell us the complete story.

How can a person of faith refuse to consider how God is personal when God was apparently deaf to the cries of people in Indonesia? When life knows little but suffering and more suffering, where then is the God who watches over his children? If God personally participates in our lives, then why the feelings of loneliness, despair, and abandonment during perilous and dark times?

We are perplexed by the idea of a God who is viewed as intimately involved in human affairs but allows the good to be trampled down by the evil or the innocent to be destroyed for no reason. If there is a God who cares, then where is the evidence? There are valid reasons for people of faith to question how or even if God is involved in our lives.

As a pastor I listened to numbers of people who felt deceived by God or who had just given up on faith. Some of these people lived in chronic pain, others were born with debilitating physical challenges, and still others were victims of the savage injustices of life. Their grievances against God were seldom malicious. Mostly these people were filled with sadness, a kind of melancholy, much like the feeling one has when an old friendship dissolves for no apparent reason. Most people find no joy with their lost confidence in God, only sorrow. Within their hearts there may still burn an ember of faith, but day by day that cinder glows more dimly, and in the absence of its warmth a cold indifference takes its place as God slides into the world of childish memories, an enchanted world of a more naïve time. I have often been present with these people as they shared their frustrations and heartache, and I have raised my own voice with them in silent protest. The unyielding misery that some people endure in this life can be gut wrenching.

I BELIEVE; HELP MY UNBELIEF

I, too, question the personal nature of God, something that has caused me to reevaluate my faith over and over again, to reexamine Scripture and study anew the teachings of the church. The God question is a difficult one, one that I have wrestled with for much of my life. I tried to be transparent and honest about my faith journey in the churches I served, but there were people under my care who were frightened by my refusal to rubber stamp handed-down traditions. Some of these people moved to other congregations where a more optimistic or doubt-free faith was espoused as the only acceptable faith perspective.

I was heartened, however, that a surprising number of people were drawn to a pastor who acknowledged his own spiritual struggles. These people identified with me and sensed that their faith journey was similar to mine. They found more fulfillment in a faith that questions than a faith that embraces God without reservation.

We more skeptical believers are like the man in Mark's Gospel who believes and yet admits to unbelief as well. Is it possible that both belief and unbelief are woven seamlessly into the same fabric of faith? Might these separate threads be stitched together in order to knit a more resilient faith? If that is the case, then doubt and unbelief are not causes for fear but serve an important role by pushing us to evaluate honestly all faith claims. If we are in some way created in the image of God, as I believe we are, then a thoughtless and uninformed faith cannot possibly honor our Creator.

I recognize that some communities of faith are uncomfortable with those who question traditional understandings of the personal nature of God. People who do not subscribe to popularly accepted patterns of belief are often perceived as threats to the more traditionally minded. It is feared that if one pillar of faith collapses the entire edifice will crumble.

A number of years ago I attended a Bible study class where the topic focused on whether God's existence could be proven. As the class weighed the pros and cons of various theistic arguments, a young woman raised a rather strong objection as to the appropriateness of the discussion.

"Why are we wasting time talking about whether God exists?" she blurted out. She continued to speak with rising conviction in her voice, "The Bible says only fools doubt the existence of God. God lives within my heart and I speak with him every day. God guides my life, my every decision. I know God is real."

Her words were spoken with sincerity and passion. Several members nodded in agreement and some commented that they, too, had never seriously grappled with the God question.

Not a single person in the class uttered a dissenting view. I knew, however, there was at least one person in the class who could not speak with such certainty. She caught my eye and her steady gaze pleaded with me to say something, to speak up for those who did not share such an optimistic and cheerful attitude that God's nature was self-evident. Several times over the previous year she had visited with me to discuss her troubled faith journey.

Her hesitancy about God represents a growing number of people within the faith community. These more hesitant believers want to be a part of the community of faith but wrestle with what it means to be in relationship with God. They feel uneasy whenever God is enthusiastically championed with bold and confident assertions. The assured absolute certainty expressed by a large population of Christians forces more cautious believers to conclude they are either defective believers or maybe even heretical.

While faith in a God who is directly and personally engaged in our lives may be self-evident to some people, an increasing segment of the religious community is moving further away from the idea that God micro-manages the world, steering the course of events to the advantage of believers and the disadvantage of unbelievers. In the face of gross injustices and incomprehensible suffering, the traditional belief in a personal God, at least in the way this idea has been popularly understood, creates conflict within the minds and hearts of a wide spectrum of thoughtful and sensitive people.

NO SPIRITUAL GIANTS

An older rabbi became a mentor to me when I was a young pastor and took an interest in my spiritual journey even though we pursued different religious paths. On occasion my wife and I attended Jewish services and worshipped with the rabbi and his wife. They were a kind and generous couple with a sincere love for God and people.

One day over lunch I asked my friend if he ever doubted the existence of God. Without hesitation he replied, "Every single day!" His response was emphatic. He stressed that faith in God continued to be an ongoing challenge for him; he wanted to drive home the point that there are no spiritual giants, only men and women of clay grappling with faith in a confusing and unfair world.

The devoted rabbi was not the only one who struggled with the God question. Over the years I have spoken with megachurch pastors, priests, rural ministers, and even denominational leaders who identified with the rabbi. They came from a wide variety of theological perspectives and a particular label like conservative or liberal didn't make faith any easier when the bottom fell out of their world. At one time or another many of us have felt that God was uncaring, remote or even non-existent. Given the right circumstances the most resolute faith can wobble and eventually splinter when faced with the fierce headwinds of life as it is on earth.

What should be subjects much discussed in circles of faith—doubt, anger directed toward God, divine neglect and abandonment—are frequently off-limits. Too often members and especially ministers who reveal chinks in their spiritual armor are marginalized or even dismissed as frauds or hypocrites. A minister who confesses to serious doubts may be placed on extended leave or terminated. If we question traditional interpretations of how God is personal or raise voices of dissent with established doctrines, such as the faithfulness of God, we may be pushed to the fringes of church membership. If we confess to a habitual absence of God's presence in our lives, we may be viewed with suspicion and if we dispute God's goodness and reliability, we could become objects of pity or branded borderline agnostics.

As I hope to show in the following pages, biblical faith leaves room for those of us who cannot buy into these cherished doctrines. An authentic faith does not require us to toe the line on these so-called orthodox positions. Moreover, we can be encouraged that the Bible embraces those who reject the party line or deny a unified and consistent picture of the nature of God.

Dissenting voices may represent a minority in the faith community, but their testimony to God's mysterious nature reverberates throughout Scripture. Their faith experiences serve to counter the standard confession that God attentively watches over and shields from harm those who trust in God. Many biblical voices tell of a more restrained and elusive God who works far more subtly in the creative process, and these confessions hold more optimistic believers accountable for their claims of an easily accessible and knowable God, and provide room for those who teeter in their faith convictions between belief and unbelief.

More skeptical attitudes are not prescriptive for every faith journey. Yet, Scripture supports a faith journey that travels through a variety of stages where suspicion and even prolonged doubt are not only indicative of authentic faith but are honored and valued by the believing community.

Faith and doubt, optimism and pessimism, joy and complaint, presence and absence are all part of the faith story. The nature of our common humanity suggests that any approach to God minus thoughtful curiosity and critical reflection may lack the necessary integrity basic to authentic faith. According to the biblical story human beings are of infinite worth and have standing before God that invites, even encourages, questioning, debate and disagreement.

I have spent my adult life as a pastor, trying to help people understand that life is lived best with God, yet I have empathy for people who respond negatively to the idea of a God who directly orchestrates events or those who have turned away from any religious commitment altogether. For innumerable people in today's world, religion holds little relevance and the church exists primarily as a cultural memorial to a more intellectually primitive time. Often people who are on the sidelines of faith, who question the creeds and dogmas that define modern orthodoxy, most of which were formulated centuries after the biblical era, are not antagonistic toward God, but are put off by narrowly constructed parameters as to what constitutes biblical faith and an almost arrogant attitude of familiarity with God.

What if there is a larger and more inclusive faith perspective, one that is rooted in the Bible, but reveals a faith journey that travels back and forth between belief and doubt? Perhaps there is a faith response, supported by Scripture, that makes room for people who question or are even skeptical of traditional interpretations of how God is personal, or even for those who have consciously attacked God during trials of unbearable suffering and then have hidden for fear of divine retribution.

By listening to biblical voices of revered personages who raised similar sensitive issues, we gain insight that both Israel and the church are sympathetic to those of us who exist in the shadow of faith, whose experiences with God reflect ambivalence, distance and feelings of betrayal. If these faith experiences can be shown to be authentic expressions of what it means to live life with God, then the door swings open to countless closet believers who have remained outside the faith community primarily because they felt unworthy or unwelcomed.

An argument can be made that God is personal and caring, but, perhaps, not in the way these qualities have been bandied about in much of the modern church culture. A number of faith stories in Scripture, when examined closely, uncover surprising insights and challenges to a religious culture accustomed to casual familiarity with God.

The Bible preserves diverse faith narratives that shaped both Israel's and the church's understanding of God. The faith community has had centuries to debate and scrutinize the reliability of these testimonies. Unfortunately, in today's church culture a myopic vision frequently restricts our ability to see beyond the large print of our comforting verses of consolation. Too often faith communities jump onto the latest popular fad promising God's nearness, dependability, and blessing when in fact bowing to the latest cultural whim may lead only to a spiritual mirage.

Over a lifetime of ministry I have observed and listened to both confident and distraught believers. Through these everyday encounters I came to realize only a slender thread separates belief from unbelief, hope from hopelessness. The most fervent believer may be only one tragedy away from crossing the line to unbelief, and the most ardent skeptic only a God moment away from acknowledging divine mystery. Faith has a fragility that defies absolute certainty regardless of which side of the divide one stands.

A prominent businesswoman asked me several years ago at a Rotary meeting why I became a minister. She was in her early forties and had in just a few short years acquired a reputation as an up-and-coming executive with a promising future. We visited for several minutes about our families and jobs. I listened as she told me of her difficult climb up the corporate ladder. "It's a hostile environment," she said, "and if your spine isn't made of steel, you'll never make it."

Soon the formal presentation began and we broke away from our conversation. After the meeting we walked together toward the exit, and just as we parted to go our separate ways, I said, "You asked me why I became a minister."

"And you never told me," she replied.

"Well," I responded, "I became a minister because spines aren't made of steel."

Neither is faith.

CHAPTER 3

SEASONS OF FAITH

Doubt and despair are not mere side-steps in an otherwise optimistic faith.
They are in fact integral to the faith experience.

- Samuel Balentine

The similarities and differences that exist among human beings fascinate me. In so many ways we share common bonds. We want to feel safe; we desire to love and be loved in return; we need a future to look forward to; we long to be fulfilled as human beings; and, well, the list goes on. Myriad human traits link us together as one family. We may have variations in the hues of our skin; our languages and cultures may sound and look nothing alike, but within each human heart there beats the longing for a meaningful and hopeful life.

Still, there are also remarkable differences. Each of us has a unique psychological make-up, and we have a wide range of emotional triggers and personalities. Some people are wired for technical abilities, while others are gifted poets or artists. One person may naturally feel compassion for disadvantaged people, yet someone else from the same family may fail to sympathize with those born with fewer assets. One child may possess innate talent for music; another child may excel in academics. Psychologists have long recognized that personality traits vary from one individual to the next in the way we think, feel, and behave. As a pastor I have observed that distinctive character features are also noticeable when it comes to faith personalities as well.

One Monday morning my assistant, a bright and deeply committed Christian, asked if she could speak with me about the previous day's message. Anticipating that she was going to toss out a compliment (something pastors desperately need on Monday mornings!), I eagerly said, "Yes."

Well, I should have made my scheduled rounds visiting sick members in the hospitals! She immediately took issue with my sermon, saying that I had been unfair in explaining the life of faith. The previous day I had spoken about how for some people faith in God presents significant challenges. "Sometimes," I said in the sermon, "people find it difficult if not impossible to believe in a personal and loving God."

My assistant protested that my interpretation of faith was skewed. "I have never found belief in a personal and loving God difficult," she gently chided. "From my earliest memories God has always been there for me and I feel his presence every day and know he watches over me."

She shared with me story after story about how God had guided her and her family through one trial after another. God's presence was as personal to her as was my presence standing before her. My assistant was an intelligent and discerning believer. She majored in sociology in college and had worked with disadvantaged youth, even taught school for a time before working as a pastor's assistant. I had no reason to question her honesty or sincerity.

After our conversation I continued to think about what she had said. Faith and trust in God were not problems for my assistant. Why is it, I asked myself, that some people find relationship with God virtually second nature, while other people struggle with belief their entire lives? For my colleague, believing in a God who compassionately watches over us presented few or no difficulties. For me, on the other hand, difficulties define my faith.

During my years as a pastor I would manage my skeptical feelings by giving myself a pep talk from time to time to rid myself of any doubts or feelings of spiritual emptiness. For a while I was able to suppress these negative emotions that might call faith into question, but then an early morning call by a distraught mother whose sixteen-year-old son had just committed suicide would shake my confidence. It seemed that there were always freakish accidents or senseless deaths that would push me to second-guess traditional conceptions of God as personal and caring. A baby born with a life-threatening defect, or a catastrophic natural disaster in a densely populated area would send me into a spiritual tailspin. Unexplainable tragedies had a way of unsettling me and made it impossible to become comfortable embracing the belief that God was directly involved in each individual life.

My assistant, to be fair, knew of these events as well and was also troubled by them, but her loss of confidence in God barely registered. She went about her life with complete assurance that God in his own good time would work everything out for good. How could two people of faith have such opposite reactions?

A simple explanation might suggest that my assistant is a true believer while I am not. Some theological circles would consider my doubts and skepticism evidence that I am not a person of faith. People who have authentic faith commitments, according to this mindset, do not call into question their personal relationship with God. Is that true? Are those of us who struggle and agonize about our relationship with God actually without faith? Or maybe we are like passengers in steerage class—on board, but definitely of inferior status.

If the Bible is to be valued, however, as a reliable record of what it means to believe, then by looking closely we will discover that those who questioned their relationship with God were not relegated to a second-class citizenship. Numerous people in the Bible, many of whom are considered spiritual pillars, knew dark and lonely periods, days when God seemed far away and any sense of hope only a fleeting mirage. It may come as a surprise to some people that doubt, feelings of hopelessness, and God-forsakenness characterize long stretches of the faith journey for celebrated figures throughout Scripture. If skepticism, despair, and divine absence are signs of God's rejection, then why are so many people who exhibited these attitudes honored in the faith community?

Some of the noted biblical heroes spent much of their lives in the shadow, an obscure place between belief and unbelief. Such personages as Abraham, Isaac, Jeremiah, Job, multitudes of the psalmists, the disciples, and even Jesus knew spiritual disillusionment, divine abandonment and sometimes questioned whether God was attentive and caring. The biblical stories depict people of faith vulnerable to doubt and feelings of hopelessness, just as so many of us are. But in spite of their vacillating faith expressions, the

Bible reveals a God who is patient and understanding, even with those whose praise was often muffled by doubt. Just because biblical figures swung back and forth between belief and unbelief, between experiencing God as personal or feeling spiritually alone, didn't mean that their faith experience was in any way of lesser quality.

It may not be a matter of intelligence, spiritual maturity or some concept of predestination that determines our sense of closeness with God. Our relationship with God may be based more on how we are wired. Some people may find intimacy with God an easier step than others. The American psychologist of religion William James studied the religious emotions of people from various faith backgrounds and determined that religious dispositions are inherently genetic. In his important book *The Varieties of Religious Experience* James concluded that people are born with certain predetermined personality traits that largely shape their religious outlook. Some people tend to be innately more hopeful and trusting, which makes religious belief less challenging; other people enter the world with a more analytical and skeptical mindset, which makes faith a more uphill climb.

James acknowledged that through dramatic life-changing events a person of one disposition may cross over to the opposite one as these inherent psychological make-ups are not static categories. A person may be genetically geared toward a more trusting attitude but may slip over to a more skeptical frame-of-mind depending on circumstances and vice-versa. Life has a way of breaking down the strongest character or buoying the most cynically downtrodden. Simply put, genetic dispositions are not inflexible categories but merely indicate general tendencies that may be altered one way or another through life experiences.

So, is James on to something? Are people born with particular dispositions that make religious faith easier for some and more challenging for others? Do people come into the world with a greater or lesser appetite for trusting God? Does James' analysis help explain why we are the way we are?

Theologian Martin Marty sees in these two psychological dispositions similarities with faith expressions in the Bible. In his book *A Cry of Absence*, a study of the Psalms, Marty observes that the poets of Scripture reflect distinct religious attitudes. There are psalmists who confess to a faith that is hopeful, comfortable with trusting God, and less prone to doubt. According to Marty, however, there are also psalmists who struggle with accepting the orthodox position of a God who is caring and attentive. These testimonies are more cautious in trusting God and less certain of divine presence. Marty refers to these two disparate faith perspectives as "seasons of faith" and, in

Marty's study, both represent authentic experiences of what it means to believe in God. The more sanguine season Marty designates as summery faith and the more suspicious season as wintry faith. He doesn't delve into whether the two unique attitudes are genetic, but he writes that within the biblical framework these two perspectives exist side by side.[1]

Marty recognizes that within both summery and wintry experiences there are wide variations where people of one faith season may identify with the other faith season to a greater or lesser degree. Simply put, summery and wintry designations are merely convenient labels as people generally lean toward a more affirming faith or a more skeptical one.

TWO BIBLICAL APPROACHES TO FAITH

I found both summery and wintry people in the churches I served. To think that one faith disposition was more committed to God would be a mistake, for in both faith expressions there are people who strive to please and serve God, and while they experience the personal nature of God in different ways, neither the summery nor the wintry attitude has a greater or lesser commitment. The two seasons of faith bear witness to how people perceive their relationship with God, not just in the Psalms, but, as we will see later, throughout Scripture.

Summery Faith

The summery faith represents people like my assistant, people who find relationship with God to be almost second nature. Their faith experiences express confidence that God is directly involved in their lives and know more joy than grief, more optimism than pessimism. Furthermore, people of summery faith believe God interacts with them through prayer, meditation, and other spiritual exercises in a personal and direct manner. This faith disposition acknowledges that pain and suffering are realities but views these cases as anomalies, a result of faithlessness or disobedience or simply the result of a fallen world. When some horrific event or illness or catastrophe intrudes into their lives, summery faith may interpret these incidents as in some way part of God's master plan. Summery oriented people do not allow themselves to get bogged down in the nitty-gritty of life's tragedies. Evil is a harsh reality that has no easy answer and the only recourse is to trust God.

Summery inclined people do not attend church to be reminded of how difficult life is; they come to celebrate the goodness of God and to be encouraged and strengthened as they live life with God. Summery faith people enjoy divine intimacy, certainty in their religious convictions, and the promise of God's protection.

Even though a summery disposition may sound shallow and contrived to people of the wintry perspective, I am not dismissive of this attitude. In fact, respected biblical scholar Walter Brueggemann considers the "core testimony" of Israel's faith to closely resemble a summery faith. The central message of Israel's witness is that God is dependable, faithful and accessible—all characteristics of a summery disposition.[2] A passage like Exodus 34:6 typifies the summery season:

> *The Lord, the Lord,*
> *a God merciful and gracious,*
> *slow to anger, and abounding*
> *in steadfast love and faithfulness (NRSV).*

In this passage the Bible represents God as trustworthy. Moreover, God maternally cares about God's children, as the word "merciful" is derived from the noun "womb," implying motherly concern. Summery faith affirms that those who trust God will never be abandoned and God's generous and loving nature can be counted on. This promise is deeply reassuring to people and offers hope when we are in the low places of life.

Psalm 91 promises protection as God commands angels to stand guard over God's children and ward off any possible evil. The psalmist writes:

> *No harm will befall you,*
> *no disaster will come near your tent.*
> *For he will command his angels concerning you*
> *to guard you in all your ways.*
> *(Ps. 91:10-11 NIV)*

These verses offer assurance that God is actively engaged in watching over the faithful, protecting them from all harm. The theme of God's attentive concern and tender care over the upright and obedient courses through many of the psalms and has made these ancient Hebrew prayers and praises beloved by countless people through the ages.

Of course, as Psalm 1 makes clear, God's shield of protection is only guaranteed for those who follow God's laws: "For the Lord watches over the way of the righteous, but the way of the wicked will perish" (Ps. 1:6 NIV). The theological belief that only the wicked suffer continued to find support up to the time of Jesus and continues even to the present day.

People of faith draw comfort and assurance from these psalms that depict life in such unambiguous terms—obey God and enjoy God's blessing of protection, but disobey and a life of ruin will surely follow. The world is governed, according to the summery understanding, by God's steady and dependable hand, and in this ordered world good unfailingly triumphs over evil.

Wintry Faith

In most faith communities the summery disposition is touted as the normative model for people of faith. Yet, in every faith community there are those who believe in God, but whose experiences with God know more uncertainty than certainty, more twilight than sunlight, and more divine aloofness than intimacy. Wintry faith people's relationship with God is more opaque, characterized by less trust and more suspicion. Just as the season of winter ushers in shorter days and colder temperatures, wintry faith knows more shadow and less warmth. When wintry faith people see misery and injustice they cannot simply write it off as some hidden divine plan. These people resonate with Ivan in Dostoevsky's classic *The Brothers Karamazov*, who believed that if the price of heaven involves the suffering of just one innocent child, then the price is too high.

Wintry inclined people may long for God, but their faith is burdened by skepticism and doubt. They are open to the reality of God but find the reality of the world, with its incomprehensible suffering and inhumanity, profoundly unsettling and wrestle with how or even if there is some divine master plan in the universe. In spite of their misgivings about God wintry people often participate in a faith community because they value fellowship with others, and continue to believe that God's presence may be experienced, but in ways that are more subtle and less direct than what the summery disposition confesses.

Why would anyone be drawn to wintry faith? Maybe this more muted faith perspective describes their own faith journey with more honesty and presents a more complete picture of their life with God. By nature many people are more suspicious and cautious in welcoming a religious belief that defines relationship with God solely in intimate and familiar terms that run counter to much of what they have seen in life.

While wintry faith may make people of summery faith uncomfortable, there is biblical support for this more restrained faith understanding. Scripture abounds with witnesses who describe their faith journey in terms that closely align with this darker and colder season, a season of longer nights and days filled with emptiness. Multitudes of voices mired between belief and unbelief tell of their ambivalent spiritual experiences, and their testimonies appear throughout the Bible and should be valued as trustworthy expressions of what it means to live life with God.

In addressing this murky season Brueggemann writes that Israel was never completely comfortable with a totally optimistic portrayal of God. There were innumerable times in Israel's faith journey when God did not intercede on their behalf, instances when God did not protect them from evil. Brueggemann writes: "Israel's lived experience [with God] appears to deliver neither viable life-order nor generous compassion—certainly not by highly visible, nameable acts of intervention."[3] Succinctly put, Israel experienced disappointment with God, even abandonment! Israel knew times when God was not reliable, dependable or faithful and there were more than a few cases when God just didn't show up! Long ago Israelites cried out in prayer:

How long, O Lord? Will you forget me forever?
How long will Thou hide your face from me?
How long must I bear my pain in my soul
and have sorrow in my heart all day long?
How long shall my enemy be exalted over me?
(Ps. 13:1-2 NRSV)

My God, my God, why have you forsaken me?
Why are you so far from helping me,
from the words of my groaning?
(Ps. 22:1 NRSV)

Rouse yourself! Why do you sleep, O Lord?
Awake, do not cast us off forever!
Why do you hide your face?

Why do you forget our affliction and oppression?
(Ps. 44:23-24 NRSV)

Wintry faith people commiserate with these soulful pleas. Haven't many of us felt at times that God was distant or disinterested in our troubles? Haven't we tasted the bitterness of inexplicable tragedy or known someone who has? Maybe chronic sickness and declining health have wrecked our lives and we feel as though God doesn't care. Why does God abandon us in our time of greatest need? These feelings of God's indifference to our struggles can't help but raise serious questions concerning how or even if God is personal.

Marty's description of wintry faith, coupled with the biblical witness, describes the faith experiences of multitudes of people I have pastored over the years. These people often feel as though a dark cloud hovers over their religious experience. While a person of summery faith might dismiss these feelings as simply marks of chronic depression or maybe unconfessed sin, surprisingly few people of these more melancholic faith stories would agree. Only in matters of religious faith do they struggle with doubt, loneliness and despair, while in other areas of life, they meet the daily challenges with confidence and conviction. But when it comes to matters of faith, these same people feel as though they live in a shadow, a place where darkness describes their experience more than light.

As a pastor I understand that many people identify with this bleaker perspective. They may think they are alone, that something is amiss with their faith, but be assured, they are in good company. We might be shocked to discover how many people there are who struggle with faith in a personal God. They may be reluctant to admit such confessions, but they sit in the pew next to us on Sunday, work in the office with us, attend sporting events with our children, pray with us, and even live in the same household with us. They live quietly with their deep-seated sense of spiritual void, embarrassed to share their feelings for fear they will be ridiculed or rejected. The world is full of people who live in the shadow, believers who yearn for a touch of divine presence, yet live in this darker season of faith.

In July of 1959 a woman named Agnes Gonxha Bojaxhiu wrote in her diary of her experience with God:

Lord, my God, who am I that You should forsake me? The child of your love—and now become as the most hated one—the one You have thrown away as unwanted—unloved. I call, I cling, I want—and there is no One to answer—no One on Whom I can cling—no, No One.—Alone. The darkness is so dark—and

I am alone.—Unwanted, forsaken.—The loneliness of the heart that wants love is unbearable.—Where is my faith?—even deep down, right in, there is nothing but emptiness & darkness.—My God—how painful is this unknown pain. It pains without ceasing.—I have no faith.[4]

The woman who wrote these heart-wrenching words is better known as Mother Teresa of Calcutta. Her sense of God's abandonment lasted for forty years! Mother Teresa was not a substandard or inferior believer. She was a woman of remarkable faith, but her faith experience knew more darkness than light, more absence than presence. This candid admission of life in the shadow by a person of such undeniable faith and virtue gives encouragement and credibility to those of us who would unhesitatingly affix our signatures to her diary entry.

THE VALUE OF LIFE IN THE SHADOW

Every Sunday morning I faced an audience with various faith personalities. It was a difficult if not impossible assignment to connect to the wide range of faith dispositions. The believers who leaned toward the summery disposition outnumbered the wintry believers, as I well knew, but I also recognized that I could not ignore the more skeptical side for at least two reasons: First, to play it safe and only affirm the more positive perspective would not be true to my own spiritual experience. I had grown to believe that the traditional understanding of how God is personal, while containing elements of truth, and certainly comforting and appealing, was not the way many people in the Bible related to God. Secondly, by speaking only messages of comfort and cheer I would put the more optimistic believer at risk. Life is miserably unfair and sooner or later the season of shadow works its way into everyone's life, and when darkness descends upon a person's life, a perpetually optimistic and cheerful faith may be caught unprepared and abruptly turn cold toward God. Besides, as Frederick Buechner reminds us, "it is our hopelessness that brings us to church . . . and any preacher who, whatever else he speaks, does not speak to that hopelessness might as well save his breath."[5]

It is not summery faith that is at issue but an unrestrained summery faith, a faith without shadow, a perspective that recognizes only the summery season as a valid expression of what it means to live life with God.

When a faith season denies the evils and ugliness of our world and is tied to an unfettered Pollyannaish attitude, faith degenerates into a cover-up, a means to avoid facing the unpleasant realities of existence.[6] If summery faith is not alerted to the possibility of winter, an overly exuberant sense of God's closeness may actually obscure a potentially deeper and more meaningful divine encounter. In the life of faith we may learn more about God, others and ourselves while in the shadow than in the light.

How or even if God interacts with human beings may never be conclusively settled while we live on earth. Life with God resides in the province of faith. The traditional teaching, however, that a healthy faith is one that enjoys an intimate relationship with God may not necessarily represent the complete story. In fact, this understanding may be a cause for some people to resign themselves to hopelessness and give up on any possible life with God. An argument can be made, however, for a relationship with God that is "personal," just not in the way it has been popularly understood. In later chapters this argument will be fleshed out in more detail.

A BIBLICAL AFFIRMATION OF THE SEASONS OF FAITH

The blunt admission in Scripture of a faith that struggles with how or even if God is personal intrigues me. Too many faith communities tend to ignore this darker and colder season, but biblical faith openly acknowledges its presence. There is much encouragement and joy in the Bible, and these instances are to be treasured, but they must not be projected as the singular faith experience, linked inextricably to the popular conception of what it means to be in a relationship with God.

The Bible is a witness to belief and doubt, presence and absence, praise and lament. Scripture does not celebrate an unceasing spiritual high. A faith darkened by shadow occupies a significant place in both testaments. Throughout the sacred writings a resilient thread of pessimism and despair is woven into the fabric of faith. If biblical faith were a weather forecast, the outlook would be partly cloudy skies with occasional sun and the possibility of intermittent storms and plunging temperatures—an unsettled weather pattern at best.

CHAPTER 4

LEARNING TO QUESTION

Anyone who does not occasionally worry
he may be a fraud almost certainly is.

- William Irwin

Sooner or later, regardless of how strong and vibrant our faith, the light will give way to darkness, and a faith that was once clear, so absolutely certain, will grow hazy, clouded by feelings of doubt and hopelessness. A young couple awakens to a quiet room and discovers to their horror a motionless baby lying in the crib. A middle-aged father in the prime of life unexpectedly collapses and dies during a routine morning jog. A tornado rips through a trailer park, blowing mobile homes to smithereens, snuffing out the precious lives of children. These tragic events, and so many others, have forced me to take off my rose-colored glasses and read Scripture with a different lens. By being present with those who had experienced the scarcely speakable truths of existence, I grew to realize that struggle, affliction, heartbreak and death are universal realities, even for people of faith. Scripture does not hide the fact that while we do not know when the shadow will edge its way into our life, there is certainty that it will. If not today or tomorrow, soon.

As a pastor I watched with sadness as church members slowly lost interest and then finally abandoned their faith community altogether when tragedy and disappointment rocked their idealistic image of God. The disorienting cruelties of life can be harsh and unrelenting, damaging or even destroying the most resilient faith. If we look to God for direct help, we may be disappointed. Unquestioned faithfulness and obedience to God do not always result in blessing and protection from nature's inexplicable assaults. To put it bluntly, good fortune does not necessarily favor the person of faith. No one is immune from adversity, and the shock to a cheerful and optimistic belief system, when exposed to unanticipated calamity, can turn our world upside down.

Late one afternoon a young surgeon dropped by my office. He and his wife had joined our congregation several years earlier and I had grown to love and admire them. After years of trying unsuccessfully to have a child, his wife finally became pregnant and gave birth to a beautiful little girl. The church rejoiced with the ecstatic parents. Every Sunday, dressed in pink, the tiny infant with curly black hair charmed the hearts of the church nursery staff. The couple's faces glowed with joy.

The moment he walked into my office I knew something was wrong. He quickly explained to me that their daughter had been diagnosed with an inoperable brain tumor. He fought back tears as he shared with me that they would keep her at home. He did not want her to die in a hospital.

It was a rainy, cold day when the baby girl passed away. The father, holding the tiny child in his arms, looked at me and said, "If only God would have given us a little help, just a little, we might have been able to save her." His voice had a discernible tremble as he rocked the dead girl in his arms and softly sang a lullaby to her.

Following the graveside service I saw the doctor and his wife less and less. When I knocked on their apartment door to check on them, no one ever seemed to be at home. I called, but no one answered. I wrote a few notes but received no response. From time to time I would bump into them at the store or a restaurant. They were friendly but never extended the conversation. I never saw them again in church.

There were probably multiple and complex reasons why the couple withdrew from the faith community. To say that their faith was not mature enough to handle tragedy would be overly simplistic. But I can't help but wonder if one factor may have been that there was nothing in their religious inventory that could serve as a resource to guide and comfort them through their journey of darkness. They were at a loss to know how to survive an experience of life that was foreign to them.

But what if their spiritual background had better prepared them? Maybe if people are warned of the possibility of perilous times, maybe if an optimistic disposition is reminded of the inevitable uncertainties of existence, much disappointment and heartache could be alleviated, certainly not eliminated but at least softened somewhat. Yes, we will still grieve when tragedy strikes and our hearts will shatter into a thousand pieces. The suffering is not less real just because we are warned that onerous days continually wait before us, but maybe, just maybe, we will not be so completely caught off guard. That sliver of forewarning may be just enough to keep us going, not that we will soar with the eagles, but maybe we will have the strength to put one foot in front of the other, to walk and not faint. Sometimes just getting out of bed can be an act of faith.

Unfortunately, in many faith communities the church calendar omits the season where gloomy days and gray skies tend to block out any sense of God's presence. As bizarre as it may sound, I have spoken to numerous people throughout my ministry who sincerely believed that sickness or misfortune were directly related to sin. In their view the closer one walks with God, the less likely the tragic interruptions to life. Apparently, to even acknowledge the possibility that spiritually bleak and barren days may be on the horizon risks unsettling people, and casts doubt on their relationship with God, a no-no in the modern world of consumer religion. Too often today's church message boldly touts an uninterrupted feel-good faith, provided you believe and hold fast to its traditional teachings that the righteous prosper, but only the wicked suffer.

On the other hand, the biblical model projects a far more uncertain faith journey. The biblical writers knew that feelings of closeness to God were only part of the story. They were focused on drawing a wider faith picture, one that included prolonged times of spiritual disillusionment. In their faith journeys days of spiritual emptiness were a fact of life, a valuable truth that balanced a sense of God's presence with the reality of God's apparent absence. They knew that faith was not an either/or proposition but drew from both confidence and doubt, optimism and pessimism. These faith perspectives were stored in a kind of spiritual journal, and when needed they were referred to and served as reminders that the more troubling and incoherent stages of faith were not only unpredictable but also certain. The Book of

Psalms, a resource of songs, prayers and confessions by the people of Israel, chronicles such a collection of more cautious faith testimonies. And, as we will see, similarly bleak faith experiences can be found throughout the Bible. These memories provide a rich repository for believers to draw on when the cycle of faith shifts to a more menacing and disturbing direction.

THE CERTAINTY OF UNCERTAINTY

From its earliest memories, Israel never sugar-coated life with God. The journey of faith has always been cluttered with challenges. When God forged a covenant with Abraham and promised him that his heirs would rival in number the stars of the heavens, the patriarch of Israel must have been overwhelmed with joy. He and his descendants were to be priests to the world and were to provide not only moral and spiritual direction but were to be a blessing to all nations of the earth (Gen. 12:3). Abraham was at the height of feeling divine presence.

To have been chosen by God for such privilege and responsibility clearly was a heady and humbling moment for Abraham. God's promise would forever mark him as a righteous man, but even in this heightened moment there were subtle hints that a shadow was already darkening Abraham's faith experience. "What can you give me?" to show that your promise is trustworthy, Abraham asked God (Gen. 15:2 NRSV). Misgivings pushed their way into his consciousness and what was once so clear started to become muddled and confused. Questions and even doubt shot holes in his spiritual high and spun him back down to earth. At the peak of his spiritual euphoria, when Abraham had been honored by God, clouds were gathering on the horizon.

"How am I to know?" Abraham further queried (Gen. 15:8 NRSV). Had Abraham not completely bought into what his heart was telling him? His experience with God grew vague, troubled by uncertainty. Later, as Abraham fell asleep a "thick and dreadful darkness came over him" (Gen. 15:12 NIV). Was Abraham's faith unraveling a bit? Was he having second thoughts about his encounter with God? What are we, the reader, to think when the biblical text acknowledges that on this spiritual peak a "dreadful darkness" enveloped him? I suppose, like many of us, Abraham's faith was a roller-coaster ride of certainty and uncertainty, belief and doubt.

Both the summery and wintry seasons were inextricably linked together in Abraham's life with God. The biblical writers intentionally portrayed both the hopeful optimism as well as the ambivalent pessimism within this man of faith. Even in the midst of what seemed to be brightness without end, storm clouds had moved across the sun, blocking the light, creating shadow.

Abraham's spiritual certainty had been slowly transformed into cautious hesitancy. He began to question and harbor reservations about his encounter with God and started to distrust what had once seemed so sure, so clear. Who can blame him? After all, he had not seen God but only heard a voice. How could Abraham possibly distinguish God's voice from all the other voices bouncing around in his head? Abraham yearned for certainty, for more conclusive evidence, but what God offered was an intuitive sense of promise. Yes, God's promise filled Abraham's heart with anticipation and hope but even then he hedges his bet: "How can I be sure?"

Abraham's suspicious nature gives credibility to the biblical narrative. If Abraham had quietly and meekly surrendered to what he was sensing, the story would have lacked the ring of truth. That he questions, debates, and struggles with his internal feelings tells me that Abraham didn't just succumb to an emotional high. The man who is honored because of his faith was also a man of spiritual discernment, and his more guarded response protected him from being swept off his feet by a burst of spiritual adrenaline. In other words, Abraham's excitement was tempered by his suspicious nature.

LEARNING TO QUESTION

Doubt was not perceived by Abraham as the opposite of faith but as a component of what it means to live life with God. Doubt became a path for a more authentic faith experience that allowed Abraham to evaluate what he was feeling and sensing with keener insight.

A faith blessed by a confident and trusting disposition, if not balanced by a critical and suspicious nature, can be woefully ill prepared for sudden and unexpected turbulence. When we experience prolonged periods of God's presence it is easy to believe that life will go on like this forever. Yet, in an unpredictable world feelings of divine presence may ebb and flow, making preparation for a changing tide essential for survival.

As a preteen my brother and I enjoyed the summer holidays, especially Independence Day, when we were allowed to buy fireworks. One Fourth of July, when I was in elementary school, a favorite uncle of mine tricked my brother and me into setting off all our firecrackers at once. He told us that if we lit just the lead fuse to the entire package, only the first several fire-crackers would explode, making a really loud bang. Naturally, almost the entire package exploded, leaving us with only a few for the remainder of the day. When we realized he had misled us we were furious. What had been anticipated as a day of fun now became one long boring summer afternoon. My uncle, on the other hand, was thrilled. He could spend the rest of the day lounging quietly in his hammock without the exasperating noise of fire-crackers being set off every few seconds.

The memory stands out because it was the first time I remember being deceived by an adult. Up until that moment I had assumed that when adults told you something, it was true. After that epiphany I realized that even the most trusted loved ones may not be bearers of facts. From that moment forward doubt and suspicion would take on a more important role as filters of the information that came my way. Of course, I didn't fully understand all that was involved in what it meant to think critically, but that experience gave birth to an inchoate sense that not everything was as it seemed. Through the years I would continue to be fooled, caught off guard and experience awkward situations, but slowly I learned to better process information and evaluate its credibility.

As children grow older and begin to intellectually and emotionally mature, they learn gradually to discern the data that comes their way. They weigh ideas and sources of information for their reliability. Toddlers do not have these powers of discrimination. They are dependent on authority figures who provide guidance in making sense out of the vortex of voices swirling around them.

Children who are raised in healthy environments develop dispositions of credulity and simply accept the world narrative told to them. When they are told there is a Santa Claus or Easter Bunny or Tooth Fairy, they believe without question. In time they figure out how to separate what is real from what is unreal, gaining experience, insight, judgment and abstract thinking abilities.

Later on parents encourage their children to think for themselves, to be independently minded. "Don't do what everybody else is doing," they warn. "Decide for yourself." Slowly the child cultivates his own mind and is introduced to math and science, philosophy and psychology and forms mental tools to think critically and analytically. A student considers the evidence of a scientific experiment or a philosophical conundrum. Another student begins to doubt that she is using the correct algebraic equation for a particular problem. An important stage of intellectual growth is learning to critically examine the data given to us.

Doubt, suspicion, and skepticism as well as other interpretive intellectual tools allow us to grow as human beings, beings who have been created
with remarkable gifts, gifts that in some way identify and connect us to God.

Surprisingly, for a lot of us religion represents a different category. In
this area alone we are told to put our critical thinking skills on hold. "Religious tradition is sacred and untouchable," we are reminded. We are cau-
tioned against questioning God or doubting the reliability of the Bible. We
are instructed that faith is the unquestioning acceptance of what we cannot
rationally understand. To doubt religious dogma is a slippery slope that leads
to spiritual ruin.

During my years in the pastorate I was often disheartened that so many
Christians lived in a religious ghetto. In other fields—technical, scientific
or medical—these believers may have been highly trained and discerning,
but when it came to religion, they had the credulity of children. They might
disagree or debate a particular interpretation, but seldom would they call
into question a time-honored dogma or creed. Certain beliefs were fixed and
immutable.

Why would bright and well-educated people jettison their natural curiosity in matters of religious belief? Why would one's personal belief system
be off-limits to the scrutiny that is routine in other areas?

THE NEED FOR SECURITY

Perhaps part of the reason for our uncritical acceptance of religious
belief is the highly complex world in which we live. We yearn for one area
in our lives that is stable and dependable, and religion can easily become
the fallback position where we feel comfortable and secure in a volatile and
frightening world.

Ernest Becker's book *The Denial of Death* argues that the desperate need
for security is the primary reason why we find it difficult to reflect critically
on religious matters. Becker points out that people turn to religion as a way
to protect themselves from an intolerably violent and hostile world. Becker
observes that within the animal kingdom only the human being fully per-
ceives his fragile place in nature, for the human being alone is aware of his
mortality.

Animals live by instincts in a tiny fragment of the world. They do not think about tomorrow or what tomorrow might bring. They do not worry about death, illness, loss of job or any other of a multitude of disturbing aspects of life that humans face on a daily basis. Becker writes, "[A human being] not only lives in this moment, but expands his inner self to yesterday, his curiosity to centuries ago, his fears to five billion years from now when the sun will cool, his hopes to an eternity from now. He lives not only on a tiny territory, nor even on an entire planet, but in a galaxy, in a universe, and in the dimensions beyond visible universes. It is appalling, the burden that man bears, the *experiential* burden."[1] Becker reasons that the seemingly infinite expanse of space and our uncertain place within it can have a demoralizing effect on us. Even the self-confident Teddy Roosevelt was reported to have been so overwhelmed with feelings of insignificance when he considered the starry heavens, he hurried inside the house, where his world became much more manageable.

Only we human creatures comprehend our tenuous place in the world. Every day is a struggle for survival and to endure we have to adapt to the reality of our terrifying environment. The two great fears that obsess us are the day-to-day challenges of living and the looming certainty of death. In order to cope with these existential threats we develop defensive mechanisms that repress our anxieties. These defensive tools, according to Becker, "allow [a human being] to feel that he controls his life and death, that he really does live and act as a willful and free individual, that he has a unique and self-fashioned identity, that he is somebody—not just a trembling accident germinated on a hothouse planet. . ."[2]

There are countless distractions we embrace to avoid facing threats to our existence. Any commitment, passion or addiction can serve as a form of escape—sex, drugs, sports, politics, materialism, and especially religion. Anything to keep us from thinking about how fragile and insecure our place is in the world. All of these buffers protect us from being obsessed with how vulnerable we are to an assortment of dangers.

The most important of these defensive tools or mental shields is religion. Religious belief provides not only meaning to life but hope beyond death. In a chaotic and changing world, religion softens the blows inherent to our existence, both now and in the future.

Becker refers to these defensive mechanisms as "vital lies" because they are employed to mask our fear of reality. Becker is not necessarily making a value judgement on the vital lies we tell ourselves. He is not categorically saying these tools have no intrinsic worth or that they are solely illusions. Vital lies may incorporate reality, but their primary purpose is to supply a stable and secure foundation in a topsy-turvy world. The need to create buffers, according to Becker, serves to block life's overwhelming anxieties and to keep us from falling into despair.

Obviously, the term "vital lie" can be offensive to people of faith. Is Becker saying that our religious belief is fraudulent, a fantasy we concoct so we can sleep at night? Maybe it depends on how our religious shield is deployed. Religion can be and often is used as a retreat from living in an ominous world. I have known people who clung to religion to avoid facing unpleasant truths the way a drowning man desperately grabs for anything thrown to him, be it a life vest or an iron weight. Religious belief can construct a wall that keeps the world with all of its uncertainty at bay, and when religion becomes only a means to avoid facing life's calamities, then it conveniently becomes an escape from what we fear, a comforting lie we tell ourselves.

From time to time we hear a news report of a religious group that has isolated itself in some remote area, far away from other human beings. By separating from secular influences, the group believes it can lead a more righteous life, and by withdrawing from the world this religious sect doesn't have to wrestle with the knotty and perplexing problems created by a pluralistic society. When religion is manipulated in order to avoid problems, it descends to the level of fantasy, a cushion of self-deception that absorbs the blows inflicted by an indifferent world.

Religion can seduce us into creating an illusory world where we see only what we want to see and hear only what we want to hear. T.S. Eliot whimsically writes, "Humans cannot bear too much reality."[3] Indeed, a religious life can be an incredibly insular one, but it doesn't have to be.

In my experience religious belief can be much more than simply an escape from reality. Quite the contrary, religious belief can help us see reality more clearly. Biblical faith does not advocate sticking our head into the sand in order to ignore the inconvenient truths of existence. The biblical writers were well aware of the gross injustices and harrowing tragedies inherent to life, and their worship of God was not a way to ignore these existential threats but was rather a means to confront the threats head-on. Life with God inspired Israel and the church to grapple with life's inequities, to serve as active participants in bringing tangible relief to those who suffered, spiritually, physically and materially. A commitment to God can open our eyes to the way the world is and compel us to make it better.

There is a distinct difference between a religious group that intentionally avoids facing the frightening truths of existence and a religious community that intentionally confronts them. One group cordons itself off from evil, while the other group engages evil to redress as much pain and suffering as possible. One group denies difficulties with the God question, while the other group doesn't shy away from tackling the most disturbing issues of our existence with honesty, intellectual curiosity, and humility. The people who attempt to avoid reality announce, "Fear not; trust in God and he will see that none of these things you fear will happen to you." The community of faith that immerses itself into the cauldron of unexplained suffering proclaims, "Fear not; the things you are afraid of are quite likely to happen to you, but you are not alone. When we are together, we can find our way even through the darkest shadow."

One religious belief is merely a form of escape, while the other religious community recognizes life's dangers but chooses to invest itself in the messiness of life. One religion wallows in its fantasy, fulfilling the cynic's suspicion that religious belief is only an evasion from the cruel facts of life, while the other religious community transcends the self-deceit by focusing on the very dangers and concerns intrinsic to human existence. In the process Becker's vital lie is transformed into a "vital truth," a way of life that bravely faces the world, not by repressing fears, but by facing fears with courage and hope.

The religious group that devotes itself to a vital lie traffics in false hope, which eventually will be exposed, leaving people utterly hopeless. On the other hand, the community that throws itself into life's daunting challenges by doing what is right and good becomes a source of hope for dispirited people, people who yearn to make a difference and people who place the search for truth above a religion that prioritizes comfort and security.

Because a faith that engages with the world entails risk and the potential for being wrong, life with God resembles a hazardous voyage more than an anchored ship in a safe and protected harbor. An adventure on rough seas with uncertain weather has no predetermined outcome. We may shipwreck against the hidden shoals or we may founder in the dark depths of the sea. A voyage has much in common with the life of faith as both travel a hazardous course. Still, no matter how uncomfortable or what difficulties we encounter along the way, the pursuit of truth must be our highest goal, otherwise the voyage becomes a sham, a pleasure cruise in a make-believe world. Life with God is not a path to avoid life's unsavory aspects, but is a journey of continual discovery, surprise and risk. We never know what is just beyond the horizon.

There are many challenges when we dare to live life with God. Perhaps the most severe test is that we must be willing to hold gently the reins of faith, avoiding the instinct to clutch them desperately with both hands. Holding on too tightly diminishes the opportunity for spiritual vitality and growth. Faith must be given free rein because whenever we attempt to control faith, then faith stops dead in its tracks. Without flexibility and freedom, life with God becomes merely a religious exercise, an exercise without risks but also one without discovery.

GROWING PAINS

Three or four weeks into my first year in seminary I noticed a van being loaded next to the student dorm. I thought that maybe one of the students had had some kind of emergency and was forced to leave the school. I walked inside the residence hall and found a man about my age giving his now-empty room one last look before he left.

"Is there a problem at home?" I asked.

"No," he replied with an edge to his voice. "I'm leaving this God-forsaken place before it destroys my faith."

I wasn't sure how to respond. After a few moments, I asked if there was anything I could do and then watched as he turned and left the building and got into his van and drove off. Over the next several years I saw similar hasty departures from the seminary by students of all ages and backgrounds. Their reasons for leaving were probably varied, but I believe many of them were not prepared to let loose the reins of their faith. They wanted a theological curriculum that did not mess with their fixed beliefs. To their dismay they learned that seminary educations expose students to a wide spectrum of theological viewpoints. As professors challenge and question long-held cherished beliefs, students become aware that few interpretations about God or Scripture are written in stone.

Theological education is not for the faint-hearted or closed-minded. There were moments in seminary when I felt like my theological guts were being ripped out. I left class many days frightened and confused, but fortunately I had wonderful teachers who sympathized with what I was going through and made themselves available to discuss my bruised and wounded ego.

Seminary exposed the cracks—chasms, really—in my theological foundation. My faith was childish and naïve, based more on my cultural upbringing than a thoughtful and considered study of Scripture. For the first time I was confronted with inconsistencies and superstitions that had become unquestioned dogma in my belief system. It was a painful as well as an exhilarating experience. Beloved convictions were being peeled away, but my vision of God was being enlarged.

I discovered that God is far bigger than I had ever imagined. I learned that even among the most brilliant theologians there were more questions than answers. I became aware of the Bible's multifaceted layers of tradition with long histories of interpretation. I grew to understand that each reader approaches the biblical text with his or her own set of prejudices and biases, and I began to see how often the Bible is manipulated to advance ideological agendas, usually with tragic results. Gradually I came to realize that a healthy dose of doubt and skepticism would keep me honest because I, too, read Scripture with my own private agenda.

Augustine wrote, "God has given me a mind to place Discovery of Truth above all things, to wish for nothing else, to think of nothing else, to love nothing else."[4] The first priority of people of faith is to seek the truth, and if anything stands in place of truth, such as our pet ideologies or our cherished but unexamined traditions, then the worship of God soon degenerates into a form of self-worship. Faith that is not merely a vital lie but rises to the level of a vital truth, respects the necessity to doubt, to raise questions, and to examine the evidence. Belief or faith, by its very nature, affirms only the possibility that something may be true.

A number of years ago I read an article in the New York Times by the philosopher William Irwin, who teaches at King's College. Irwin admits that he is not a theist but also acknowledges that the God question cannot be summarily dismissed as a fable or crutch for emotionally unstable or immature people. Smug and complacent atheists are just as misguided as their theistic counterparts.

Written to both believers and non-believers, Irwin's words are thought provoking: "Dwelling in a state of doubt, uncertainty and openness about the existence of God marks an honest approach to the [God] question."[5] Irwin argues that for either perspective to insist that their point of view is the only acceptable position ignores intellectual reality. Irwin writes, "Anyone who does not occasionally worry he may be a fraud almost certainly is."[6]

Irwin's intellectual humility is refreshing. And he is right about God. God welcomes those of us who struggle with doubt or even get our theological belief systems out of whack. A relationship with God does not require absolute certainty or acing a theological examination but begins as an adventure and continues by being open to learn how God reveals divine presence in the world.

Biblical faith is not locked into any intractable belief system. The Bible recognizes that God transcends any conception we may have and any attempts to box God in, to make God accessible and predictable, as a kind of escape hatch in emergencies, have little support in Scripture. For the most part people in the Bible who pursued God were aware of the dangers, risks and challenges, as both testaments emphasize the high cost of venturing out in faith. The people of the biblical era did not understand life with God as primarily a means to avoid facing the world's uncertainties. On the contrary, the more these people grappled with God, the more their eyes were opened to the wicked absurdities and injustices of existence. Their faith provided them with the courage to confront these evils and alleviate as much heartache and misery as possible. Their faith had little about God figured out, and, moreover, they showed little interest in nailing down a litany of theological dogmas. They were more intent on following a way of life that would lead to a more human and humane world.

A human and humane world is a place where every person is valued as an image of God. The Golden Rule goes to the heart of how we are to treat each other: "In everything do to others as you would have them do to you" (Matt. 7:12 NRSV). All the world's great religions affirm this principle. Life is unfair and difficult and only by being our brother's and sister's keeper can the human race flourish.

TO WALK AND NOT FAINT

At times our life with God may feel as though we are soaring on eagle's wings, but then without warning life can turn cold and dark. We've all been there at one time or another; some of us may be there now. When life falls apart we may be strongly tempted to give up on God. Tragedy can and does call into question whether God can be counted on, and, if God is not with us when we find ourselves in the shadow, then why even bother? I cannot blame those who shrug their shoulders in quiet resignation and walk away from faith. The heavy burdens that some people bear are scarcely imaginable, and those who lose confidence in God have my understanding, not my judgement.

But maybe those who turn away are actually taking a step in the right direction! Is it possible that sometimes in order to mature in our life of faith, we must let some things go, rid ourselves of comfortable but misleading perceptions of God? Maybe some people who turn away from faith are in reality pushing further ahead, to unchartered seas, new and revealing adventures, opening the possibility of discovering more authentic ways of experiencing God's presence and grace during the more unsettling times of life.

It can be scary to push ahead. We may feel unstable and maybe even a little queasy. Our world has been turned upside down, and there may be much emptiness within, but if we can somehow manage to put one foot in front of the other, to walk and not faint, we may find that God is closer than we think.

Faith doesn't pretend to have all the answers. Anyone who exercises faith lives with a host of questions and doubts, frustrations and disappointments. Those of us who have ventured life with God face formidable challenges that force us to evaluate our faith again and again. We have learned the hard way that life with God is not so much a place to stand as it is a path to follow. If we are looking for absolute certainty, we are sure to be disappointed. Nevertheless, if we stay the course, we will participate in the greatest mystery in the universe—possible life with God.

CHAPTER 5

WHEN HOPE IS MORE THAN A WISH

But I will hope continually.

- *A Psalm*

Earlier I wrote of my assistant who knew far more sunny days than shadowy ones. A large number of people in the faith community fall into this category, maybe even a majority. While she agrees that there is much suffering and heartache all around us, she would probably add: "Look, no one doubts that on occasion bad things happen, but what are a few bumps in the road compared to eternity? Jesus suffered and died but then on the third day he arose. Any difficulties or hardships we experience now are only temporary setbacks, and then what awaits us in heaven will make these earthly trials insignificant."

From a biblical point of view there is an element of truth in this perspective. The Apostle Paul wrote in Romans that our present sufferings pale in comparison to our future life with God (Rom. 8:18). This belief has bolstered the faith of countless believers through the ages and continues to be a source of inspiration for those trapped in a maze of unescapable suffering. In trying times, if we can just hang on, then we will spend an eternity with God. Without the hope that our earthly burdens will one day be lifted and replaced by a new reality, free from the sorrows and heartaches of this world, religion would offer scant comfort.

We should not be surprised that religious skeptics have unleashed a salvo of philosophical attacks against this idea of a future hope. Because faith in God anticipates a future life free of pain and death, critics have harshly judged religion as a kind of drug that beguiles believers to ignore the ills of this world by focusing on the next. Unfortunately, this criticism has frequently been justified. The hope of a future life has often blinded the faith community to much of the ugliness that has stricken the world and our responsibility to repair it.

It may seem strange to learn that hope has not always been viewed in a positive light. In ancient Greek mythology the opening of Pandora's Box released all the evils into the world, including hope, which was seen as a curse because hope deceives. Hope, it was thought, creates an illusion that the future will somehow be better than the past, a concept that the Greek culture rejected. The philosopher Spinoza believed that hope betrayed a flaw in human character, that of yearning for that which was unattainable. Freud called hope an illusion and through therapy tried to move people away from the illusion principle (hope) to the reality principle, accepting the world as it is.

Indeed, hope can serve the same function as Becker's "vital lie," a defense mechanism that shields people from life's crushing realities. Hope, in this sense, has limited value, for its primary purpose is not concerned with this life but with a future life. Consequently, the present with all its problems and difficulties is not worth a serious investment of time, since it occupies such a short interlude before an eternity in heaven. If hope is thought of in this way, with no commitment to today, then its critics are justified to call it an illusion.

But hope, like religion, can be more than a comforting wish. There is nothing deceptive about raising expectations of a heavenly future, as long as those expectations do not abdicate responsibility to help make this world a better place now. If my hope promises me heaven but does not incentivize me to act in the present to make possible a more promising future, then my hope becomes merely a vital lie, for it does not carry the seeds that make tomorrow possible. For instance, we may hope to do well on a job interview, but if we have not prepared, then more likely than not, that hope will never materialize. We may hope to win first place in a piano recital, but if we have not practiced, we are sure to be disappointed.

Biblical hope anticipates the future but at the same time is grounded in the here and now. Abraham's vision of a future inspired him but also motivated him to keep God's covenant obligations, to do what was right and good (Deut. 6:17-18). He was compelled to live according to his understanding of God, a divine being who is compassionate, longsuffering, and just but also forgiving. Jesus envisioned a future life with God but also stressed caring for the sick, hungry, and poor. For Jesus God's Kingdom was not only a future to look forward to but was also to be experienced to some degree in the present. His teachings for the most part were oriented to how his disciples should live in this world (Matt. 5-7). Biblical hope, then, is not some pie-in-the-sky wishful projection, but presents a vision of a new tomorrow that begins with constructive actions now, encompassing both present and future.

Hope, then, functions as a kind of prologue for a better tomorrow wherever people of faith compassionately reach out to those who suffer in ways that are commensurate with our understanding of a moral and ethical God. Biblical hope is tied inextricably to today's reality as evidenced by people who engage in acts of love to minimize human suffering. In the way the Bible understands it, hope is not an escape from reality but an incentive to begin shaping a new reality.

With all due respect to the naysayers of hope, who view hope primarily as a means to avoid having to face the world as it is, hope is a necessary component for human survival—a vital truth. Without hope we lose the will to live.

On a routine basis I ministered to people who had given up on life. Usually, these people had reached an age when their bodies had deteriorated and doctors could do no more. They lived in chronic pain and depression. On numerous occasions I spent time with people who had lost their spouses after decades of marriage and no longer wanted to live, and without some morsel of hope that was tangibly connected to the present these people failed to thrive and soon died. Hope is the foundation principle of existence—it is the breath of life. Without hope we will not endure as a human species.

As people of faith we live with hope and are open to the possibility of a higher reality, but that does not mean that our present circumstances are unimportant. Unexplained tragedy and suffering continue to trouble us and are not less real just because we aspire to a future where words like evil, calamity, atrocity, sickness, and death have no meaning.

Deep down inside we know that to ignore the problems of today does a disservice to what it means to be human. Dismissing or trivializing the evils all around us by claiming these wicked absurdities are not our problem is tantamount to someone standing on the beach passively watching a young child only yards away drown in the ocean. He can hope the child is rescued, but hope without action is not only meaningless, it is contemptible.

Jesus never hid the difficult and stressful day-to-day challenges from his disciples. He believed in a future heaven, but that future was not disconnected from the present. Jesus emphasized that eternal life with God begins with a particular way of life, and his teachings accentuated how people of faith are to live in this world. A reading of the Sermon on the Mount reveals selfless principles of behavior for today: going the extra mile, loving the unlovable, forgiving our enemies, putting the lives of others ahead of our own, living simply. Jesus makes plain that hope for a future life with God actually begins in the present moment.

DIFFERENT FAITH JOURNEYS

One morning at breakfast Jesus warned Peter that obedience may not result in blessing but might, in fact, cost him his life. Jesus told Peter that his faith journey would lead him on a path he would not have chosen, and ultimately the path would "reward" him with an untimely death. When Peter shifted his glance toward the beloved disciple and inquired about his fate, "Lord, what about him?" (John 21:21 NRSV), Jesus replied that he should only be concerned about his own destiny. Tradition records that Peter was crucified upside down, an unimaginably gruesome end, while John lived to a ripe old age.

While the immediate context of this story stresses the demands of discipleship, the story also has broader implications. Some people are fortunate when it comes to their life with God. They enjoy good health and are blessed with a wealth of talents and opportunities. Others not so much. I have a friend who worries about everything and has a rather gloomy outlook on life but if you knew her story, you would more than likely be sympathetic. From her earliest memories she has gone through one calamity after another—her parents were killed when she was very young, she has undergone a variety of serious health issues, resulting in a number of disabilities, and lives in chronic pain. She has been shaped by life's tragic circumstances and views the world from that bleak perspective. When I am in conversation with her, and listen to her faith struggles, I remind myself that she has experienced so much more misfortune than I. I marvel that she continues to hang on to her faith in God, in spite of her pain-riddled life, and has chosen to live a life of faith, not as a way to escape from suffering or to spend her days fantasizing about some future world, but as a way to bear her suffering with dignity and meaning. She hopes that heaven will someday free her of pain, but she works tirelessly to assist others to find meaning in their daily health challenges. While she prays for a future without pain, her hope is rooted in making the present better. She defines biblical hope and I stand in awe of her.

LIFE PLAYS NO FAVORITES

Even for people of faith life is tragically unfair and unpredictable. The biblical writers make clear that life with God has no predetermined course. Yes, there will be times when God's presence feels palpably near and protective, but then suddenly, without warning everything can change.

Haven't we experienced similar moments when a phone call or a text or a test result collapsed our world into what seemed like insufferable chaos? Often there was no rhyme or reason, no explanation, for what befell us. It just happened.

An old friend recently called me to tell me of his wife's death. Years earlier my wife and I had been good friends with the couple. We took several ski vacations together with our children, enjoyed a number of family picnics during the summer months and after church on Sunday nights our families would frequently go out for pizza. But when I assumed the pastorate of a church in a neighboring state we gradually lost touch. I think the death of his wife stirred memories of happier times, and by reaching out to me he was vicariously reliving those cherished days.

My grieving friend shared with me that after years of hard work he and his wife had finally retired and were looking forward to travel and enjoying their time together. But not long after their retirement my friend's wife was diagnosed with multiple myeloma, and their plans dramatically changed.

Quickly, her health problems began to mount with cascading frequency. She developed Parkinson's disease that caused severe tremors in her arms and legs. She lost the ability to walk and care for herself. A woman who had always prided herself in staying fit and healthy, who served as a volunteer for church and community causes, was stricken with a terrible disease that robbed her and her family of what should have been a deeply satisfying period in her life.

"Everything happened so fast," her distraught husband shared with me, "we hardly had time to catch our breath." They went to some of the best specialists in the field, tried stem cell therapy and other cutting-edge treatments, but the disease was relentless. For a number of years their days were filled with doctor's appointments, hospital visits, tests, and countless medications. During the last eighteen months dementia set in, adding another cruel injustice to an already horrendous situation. As I listened to my friend I thought to myself, life plays no favorites.

Much like the unpredictability of life itself, there is an uncertain element in life with God—we never know from one day to the next what to expect. The uncertainty may frustrate or even repulse us. Some, living in a prolonged season of blessing, may even deny the seemingly random nature of life with God, as it cuts across the grain of much of what they have been taught. There is persistent thread in Scripture on the tangible benefits of obedience to God, where God watches over and protects us and guides our every step, even in the face of danger. When the biblical writer thanked God that he was the apple of God's eye and felt secure in the shadow of God's wings, we can assume he must have experienced some significant divine intervention in his past that led him to that assurance (Deut. 32:10; Ps. 17:8). When Proverbs teaches that right living will be rewarded in this life, there must have been some reinforcement behind this belief (Prov. 13:21; 28:25).

Israel's entrance into the Promised Land, however, reveals the flip side to the promises of God's dependability—a complete sense of divine abandonment. After decades of struggle Israel finally stepped into the land flowing with milk and honey, but instead of finding security and abundance, they found uncertainty and danger. Enemies on all sides threatened to drive them out of the land God had promised. How could God have allowed this to happen? Day after day they had to fight for survival. During an unusually difficult time, when hopelessness left the nation in spiritual turmoil, a messenger appeared to a young man named Gideon and reassured him, "The Lord is with you." Gideon is shocked. "If the Lord is with us, why then has all this happened to us? And where are all his [God's] miracles our ancestors told us about?" (Judg. 6:13).[1]

Gideon speaks for countless people who question where God is when life crashes down around them, when what they were promised doesn't materialize into reality. The euphoria that is derived from God's presence can quickly turn into pitch-black darkness when sudden, unexpected calamity forces us to rethink how God is with us or even if God is with us. How do we pray when our vision of God has been shattered by chronic suffering, when our hearts are filled with nothing but confusion, grief, and emptiness? How do we remain faithful to God when God appears distant and indifferent to our wrecked life?

One Sunday morning a young wife and mother from our church stopped to buy donuts for her Bible Study class. When she pulled out onto the street, a truck ran a red-light and slammed into the side of the car, killing her. A few hours later I stood by the side of the grieving husband as he wept over her broken body. The shock of seeing her lifeless form rendered him speechless. Her life was meaninglessly erased on her way to church. The ugliness of existence spares no one and like Gideon we wonder, if God is with us, how can these terrible things be happening? Where is God's protection that so much of Scripture promises us?

It appears that life with God doesn't serve as a vaccine that inoculates us from life's harsh and cruel truths, but by conditioning ourselves to the possibility of adversity, we may be better prepared for its inevitable assault. Be ready for a course change, the Bible warns, it is only a matter of time before you find yourself struggling to keep your head above water. We do not know the direction our life will take, whether we will enjoy a long and healthy life or be chronically burdened by life's injustices, but in all probability most of us will travel through a variety of experiences, both good and bad. It is the price we pay for being born human.

When life's sorrows become greater than we can bear, it is human nature to feel abandoned by God, as though we have been set adrift in an ocean of divine neglect. When you awaken every morning to pain, either physical or emotional, you may soon grow disenchanted with the life of faith. The disenchantment may grow into resentment and the resentment may turn into apathy or even rage. If God exists, we tell ourselves, then what difference does it make? What hope remains within us is directed toward our doctors, medicines, therapies, and technological breakthroughs, more efficacious remedies than praying to a God who appears to be absent or even worse, uncaring.

Some of us may never recover from our sense that God has left us. If the darkness lingers long enough, if the enduring pain is brutal enough, we may simply choose to live our lives apart from God. As a pastor I spoke on a number of occasions with disheartened people who had just given up on God. They had lost confidence in a God who was personal in any meaningful way. I found it difficult to even broach the God question with them. Surviving their

traumatic experience had left them confused, feeling isolated, anxious, apathetic, and they were often filled with a bitter sense of divine betrayal.

The stories of Abraham, Moses, Jeremiah, the psalmists, Job, the disciples and even Jesus tell of people who also felt that God had abandoned them,
and who, in some cases, responded by targeting God with verbal assaults, yet
these same individuals are praised for their faith. Go figure! Some of these
forlorn souls may have been close to giving up on God or maybe some did
cross the line from belief to unbelief. Only God knows. Near the end of his life
King David confessed, "Our days on the earth are like a shadow, and there is
no hope" (1 Chron. 29:15 NRSV). Why would the biblical writers have recorded such a pessimistic confession unless David had actually made it or segments of Israel had actually expressed it? Even David, whom the Bible calls a
man after God's heart, could move perilously close to crossing the line from
belief to unbelief, from hope to hopelessness.

In spite of what could be called a biblical roll of honor of those who endured trial after trial, there are many within the faith community who continue to believe that misfortune and tragedy are signs of God's judgement
and not normal parts of life with God. If they read the Bible from a narrow
perspective, cherry-picking a few verses here and there, it is not difficult to
come up with that conclusion. A case can be made that the righteous prosper
and the wicked suffer (see Psalm 1), but that does not represent a complete
picture of life with God. We have seen that the Bible does not speak with only
one voice but a variety of voices that sometimes seem wholly disparate.

Why does the Bible speak with contrasting voices? How can we balance
these contradictory messages?

We will probably never be able to completely explain these theological
contradictions, but the Lord's Prayer may offer a partial clue. In the prayer
Jesus prays for God's will to "be done on earth as it is in heaven" (Matt. 6:10
NRSV). Why would Jesus feel the need to pray these words? Maybe it was because he realized that God's will is not always done on earth. Jesus prayed in
anticipation and hope that one day both heaven and earth would align with
God's will. In the meanwhile, because we live in a world where God's will is
not always done, there is unpredictable evil and no one is spared.

Then, too, God's mysterious nature may shed light on why the Bible
seemingly speaks with two voices. God, as C.S. Lewis wrote, cannot be tamed,
managed or manipulated—God is not safe.[2] According to the prophet Isaiah,
God is elusive and at times hides himself (Isa. 45:15). When we set out to live
life with God there will be times when divine presence seems far away, and
our spiritual life empty of warmth, and feelings of hopelessness steal what-

ever joy remains. Unexplained tragedy and suffering can test the most resilient faith, and people who dare to risk life with God will be exposed, sooner or later, to seemingly endless dark and confusing days of divine neglect. We may feel as though we will never see the light again and consciousness of God's presence remains only as a distant memory.

No one complains during the tranquil and comforting days of good fortune. Few people shake their fists at God when blessing follows blessing, and there might be days like that, but eventually the calm seas turn tempestuous and life plunges into a dark and cold ocean of despair, and when that happens, we may convince ourselves like David that there is no hope.

These more unsettled times, however, can provide opportunities for us to develop into more sensitive and thoughtful people. Life in the shadow may be the perfect time for spiritual growth, opening the possibility to a more meaningful faith journey. During bleaker days, especially during these bleaker days, we can become more aware of a transformative side of faith that is often hidden from us when we revel in the comforting embrace of divine presence. Feeling exiled to the long, dismal nights of God's absence we may surprisingly see life more clearly, we may better be able to distinguish priorities from the things of lesser importance. We may become more aware of the brokenness and heartache around us that we somehow overlooked before. In the brightness of God's presence we may have been blinded by perpetual blessing and failed to notice the misery and suffering common to all too many.

I spent a good part of my ministry talking to people in hospitals, nursing homes, and rehab centers. In addition, people who had lost jobs or were struggling with a problem marriage or a rebellious teenager or had some other major or minor crisis would drop by the church to visit with me. As a pastor it didn't take me long to realize that multitudes of people face formidable challenges on a regular basis. Sharing in other people's grief opened my eyes to the daily struggles that so many people face, but my visual acuity sharpened considerably when I began to realize that my personal burdens, burdens that I often complained to God about, helped me to more easily identify and sympathize with those who were in pain, pain that often made my troubles seem insignificant. Because of my burdens I listened to their stories more attentively; I thought more deeply how I could help them; my prayers for them were more earnest and consistent, and I found myself thinking and praying for them throughout the day. Ironically, only in darkness could I see more clearly.

Secondly, as we begin to focus on others and less on ourselves, we find that we are being drawn closer to other human beings. During the carefree days when we feel particularly close to God we might deceive ourselves into thinking that we can make it alone. We convince ourselves that the only relationship that matters is the one we have with God, but the darker season of faith awakens within us the realization that we cannot survive without community. Only by linking our lives with other people can we enjoy a life that is fulfilling and hopeful.[3]

Finally, life in the shadow may uncover a spiritual life that has grown flabby and complacent. A life free of suffering and pain has a way of lulling us into thinking that our good fortune is somehow deserved, that we have earned God's favor. An unexpected medical report or some other intrusion of evil into our lives can demolish our spiritual arrogance and force us to live more humbly with God. When the journey of faith grows dark, we venture out more carefully. We are less sure of ourselves and realize that we may lose our way at any moment. We become fully attentive to the fragility of our faith, to the reality that sometimes faith is more of a question than an answer. Only when light is as darkness do we fully grasp that real faith can be both half-sure and whole-hearted.

There is nothing pleasant about life in the shadow. We do not want to be there, would do anything not to be there but there is where we are. While there may be difficult days ahead, days filled with frustration, fear or even anger, we are not without hope. Even in the darkest shadow, there is always some light.

Endless days of suffering and feelings of God's absence have a way of wearing us down. We grow weary of trying to connect with a God who doesn't seem very interested in us. We may finally conclude that "If life with God is this difficult, then why even try?" The theologian Dorothee Soelle speaks for many when she writes: "Suffering can bring us to the point of wishing that the world did not exist, of believing that non-being is better than being."[4] How do we hang on to hope when there is nothing inside of us but unending disappointment and pain? Sometimes we need a more visible source of power to give us strength to make it through just one more day.

Perhaps the Bible provides a clue. People like Abraham, Gideon, David and the disciples knew these troubling periods, but they managed somehow to continue in their faith journey. There must have been some reality that strengthened them, something tangible that gave them hope in the midst of their aching emptiness. But what was it?

During my friend Steve's battle with cancer he wrote in his blog: "I want God to stand beside me and tell me what he has in store for me. I want answers. To date, nothing." How many of us could have written those words during particularly distressing times? When our lives cratered we may not have felt that God was there for us. We rationally understand that suffering and hardship may be the price we pay for being born human, but as people of faith we believe we will not experience this darker side of life alone. Yet so often we do. Where can we find answers when God seems light years away? We may be disappointed if we expect some direct, intimate response from God. But, if we listen carefully to the voices of those who have traveled this way before, we may discover that God is closer than we think.

CHAPTER 6

YOUR OWN PERSONAL JESUS

A religion which does not affirm that God is hidden
is not true.

- Blaise Pascal

One Sunday night during a church business meeting a woman stood to voice her dissent with a recommendation from the Church Council. As I recall, it was a rather trivial matter, but she was extremely agitated. She began her comments saying something like: "I have prayed about this issue and God has told me that we need to vote down this proposal." She continued to speak for several more minutes, but I was stunned by how confident she was that God had personally spoken to her. After much discussion, and in spite of the woman's objection, the motion passed. She hurried out of the sanctuary visibly upset, and even after repeated visits by me and others, never returned.

I have no idea if God had spoken to the woman, but what I do know is that many Christians believe God directly speaks to them in private and exclusive conversations, usually not audibly but nonetheless in distinctive ways. The belief that we can enjoy an intimate relationship with God and have direct dialogue with the Almighty is embedded deeply within the fabric of the modern church. The lyrics of the Depeche Mode's *Personal Jesus* resonate with many:

> *Your own personal Jesus.*
> *Someone to hear your prayers.*
> *Someone who cares.*

To believe that God speaks to us and hears our prayers and cares about us is deeply reassuring. If God were uninvolved and disinterested in our affairs, why would we even bother with religion? If God can't be experienced in some meaningful way, then what's the point? Only a God who is somehow present with us can make a difference.

During uninterrupted days of blessing, when we feel close to God, we seldom struggle with God's personal nature. Praising God from whom all blessings flow rolls easily off our tongue. Life is good. We may even feel as though we have our own personal hotline to God. Not only are we on speaking terms with God, but we may feel as though our direct access grants us a kind of favored status.

But not everyone enjoys this experience. When our dreams turn to ashes over and over again, any positive feelings we have toward God can crumble. When a person is beaten down day after day by one ordeal after another, God can seem indifferent to our pain or even nonexistent. If we do manage to hang on to our faith, we may wonder why we live under such a curse, why has God turned away from us or even become hostile. We cry to the heavens, "What have we done to deserve the cold shoulder? What sin have we committed that has earned God's wrath? Why aren't we experiencing intimacy and blessing?"

The biblical story, however, plainly acknowledges these darker feelings of God's apparent absence, and assures us that both divine presence and divine absence represent authentic cycles of faith. Many of us have experienced that spiritual loop throughout our lives. There have been times when we sensed a closeness to God, and there have also been occasions when we felt that God was distant and remote. A problem arises when we claim one cycle more authentic than the other or our relationship with God more intimate than someone else's. The woman who claimed to have had a direct word from God was misguided on several counts, but her principle misconception lay in believing that she alone had heard from God. She was completely sat- isfied that she had privileged access to God that no one else had.

THE IMPORTANCE OF COMMUNITY

People living in the biblical period rarely understood relationship with God in such extreme individualistic terms. Today's "me first" culture is a relatively modern phenomenon. Before the Reformation of the six- teenth-century, a Christian's identity was inextricably linked to his/her community of faith. Individuals thought of themselves in relation to other people much more than we do today, and difficult as it is for we moderns to understand, the framework of a society in earlier times centered on commu- nity, more specifically the church, and not the individual.

From birth to death the community was pivotal to a person's well-being. Life was ordered by the church calendar, specifically sacred times of the year such as Advent or Lent. The life of faith was articulated through the creeds that had been shaped by earlier communities. Charles Taylor describes Christians before Luther as thinking of themselves as passengers on an ocean liner.[1] They were part of a group and shared common experiences. A person's identity was formed through his family and church, and he felt dependent on a larger network of people for survival. It was self-evident before the Reformation that no person was an island. Even an experience with God was a shared experience, primarily through the worshipping community.

The Reformation contributed to a change in how we thought of our- selves. Luther taught that a Christian is a perfectly free lord, subject to none. In Luther's view we do not need a priest to mediate a relationship between God and us because every person is his/her own priest and has access to God directly. This concept revolutionized our understanding of the self. Uninten- tionally, the Reformation not only fractured fellowship between Christians, by creating Catholic and Protestant divisions, but also paved the way for a new understanding of our identity.

After Luther's break with the Roman Church, individuals, at least in Protestant- leaning regions, slowly developed the idea that the church was no longer essential for a relationship with God. The central place of the church as a conduit between God and God's people was replaced by a believer's personal relationship with God/Jesus.

An advocate of the Reformation, steeped in the modern world of hyper-individualism, might respond, "Of course a personal relationship with Jesus does not require the mediation of the church. That was the key point of the Reformation." And he would be right, but with every step forward, sometimes we also take a step or two backward.

The Bible stresses that a life of faith begins with a personal decision and a community of faith cannot make that decision for us. The invitation to live life with God is addressed to each person, and while the church may be compared to a large ocean liner, no one is forced to board.

When we make a decision to risk faith, however, we also become a part of a larger whole. The emphasis in Scripture on love of neighbor and the importance of community recognizes that the life of faith is not a solitary journey. A relationship with God involves life with others. Asocial private piety has no support in Scripture. When Jesus teaches his disciples how to pray, he does not begin with "My Father" but rather "*Our* Father." The prayer signifies the importance of "us" and not "I." In the theology of Jesus, even prayer is a communal act. Throughout the New Testament Jesus pictures a person of faith as one who is immersed in the joys and sorrows, successes and failures, and the living and dying in community.

The Apostle Paul uses the metaphor of the body of Christ to depict the faith community (1 Cor. 12:12-31). A finger, for instance, has unique properties that define it, but separated from the rest of the body, the finger loses its reason to be. Each of us has a role but only together can we function as the church, representatives of God's presence in the world. While we stand before God as individuals, we cannot adequately fulfill our purpose as human beings apart from community.

Luther did attempt to correct what he realized was a potential danger (the practice of individual priesthood becoming a license for self-indulgence) by acknowledging that we are servants of all and subject to all. Luther recognized the need to balance personal accountability to God with accountability to each other, but the cat was out of the bag, and the excesses that Luther feared became a millstone around the neck of the believing community. What was meant to challenge us to greater personal responsibility gradually became a permission slip for each of us to go our own way and justify our actions by claiming a unique relationship with God regardless of how our actions might affect others.

The people of faith as described by the New Testament (see especially Acts 2) were bonded together through a shared understanding of what it meant to be a follower of Jesus. An individual professing faith apart from his community would have been unthinkable. After the Reformation, however, people began to see the church in a different light. The lessening of church influence gained momentum over time and continues to the present day. Where once community life revolved around the seasons of the church calendar and participation was a given, in today's average congregation church schedules are often determined by sporting events, and only about a third of the membership attend worship on any given Sunday.

The spiritual void left by a diminished church heightens our need to feel close to God since we no longer feel close to each other, and with our perceived personal and direct access to God we no longer need the church. Consequently, her traditions and teachings have become secondary factors in our lives. In contrast to previous generations of faith, where all Christians were passengers on a ship, now each of us has his own individual rowboat and charts his individual course.

The Reformation was an important corrective in the life of faith because it placed a renewed emphasis on personal decision and commitment, which had lost traction since the days of the first century church. In today's church culture, however, the pendulum has swung too far in the other direction. Individual autonomy has minimized the role and value of life together. If the church over the centuries became guilty of minimizing the importance of individual decision and responsibility, today's church culture contributes to a kind of spiritual free-for-all. Neither extreme represents a biblical model of what it means to be in relationship with God.

Long ago I made my decision to pursue life with God, and even today I continue to reflect on what this commitment means and how it guides and influences my life. I confess that after a lifetime of study, introspection and prayer, I still cannot define precisely what it means to have a "personal" relationship with God. The mystic within me cannot totally abandon the notion that something mysterious and wonderful connects me to God. At the same time my understanding of the Bible leads me to distrust any explanation that favors me over others with special privileges or private insights into God.

From my reading of Scripture, a relationship with God/Jesus compels me to identify with his way of life and try to the best of my abilities to live out his teachings in community with other human beings. Jesus points to God and directs me to live a life congruent with his earthly life. Through his teaching and example, as recorded in Scripture, Jesus encourages me to develop my moral and creative powers, which guide me to be less focused on myself and more concerned and involved with those around me.

A relationship with God/Jesus challenges me to replicate in my own life Jesus' image of God, a heavenly Father who is loving, selfless, and forgiving. I do not believe that my life with God elevates me over any other human being.[2] Instead, my faith commitment instills a conscious awareness of my responsibilities to pattern my life after Jesus. However we choose to define relationship with God/Jesus, I believe this expression refers more to responsibilities than privileges.

In the New Testament, when Jesus invited people to follow him as a pathway to God, he was calling them to a way of life that was contrary to a what's-in-it-for-me mentality. To follow Jesus requires sacrifice, self-lessness, love of neighbor, forgiveness of enemy and much more. The Jesus way is best symbolized by the cross—an instrument denoting self-denial and death to the old way of life. Jesus taught that by following the way of the cross, a rejection of a "me first" mentality, we enter into community, not only with each other but also with God. Instead of the Jesus way—a sacrificial life offered to God in service and love—too often the modern church's understanding of a personal relationship with God emphasizes personal benefits while minimizing accountability and engagement with others.

DEFINING A PERSONAL RELATIONSHIP WITH GOD

Frankly, the concept that we can enter into a personal relationship with our Creator may sound far-fetched, presumptuous and/or arrogant. How can finite creatures, frail and fallible as we are, even know, let alone experience intimacy with, the Almighty? The popular author Philip Yancey recognizes the problem and suggests a possible explanation as to how this relationship may occur. He begins by drawing an analogy between a relationship with a friend and a relationship with God.[3] According to Yancey, through intimate and varied kinds of conversations and experiences we share with each other, we learn the necessary relational tools that make relationships possible. Without engaging with other people in personal and intimate ways, we would not have the psychological or emotional resources to be receptive to, let alone seek, a divine encounter. By interacting with other human beings we unwittingly develop interpersonal skills that lay the groundwork for a possible relationship with God. But Yancey warns that even human relationships "rest on a platform of uncertainty that preserves the mysterious quality of otherness."[4] Yancey makes clear that even with other people, with close friends, for instance, we can only know them in a limited way. And God's "mysterious quality of otherness" is infinitely greater than that of any human.

While Yancey describes similarities between human relationships and a God relationship, he also acknowledges radical differences. We can visibly see, interact with and directly experience other human beings. With the mysterious and unseen God our access is more indirect, more subtle. There might be occasions when God pulls back the curtain a little to give us a better glimpse, but most of our experiences occur indirectly through church, spiritual disciplines, sacraments and, most importantly, community worship. These mediated experiences, or what Yancey calls "means of grace," imply that a relationship with God is not completely independent of the faith community. Any relationship we claim to have with God hinges on the relationships we have with each other, which means that a broken relationship with a fellow human being betrays a broken relationship with God (I John. 4: 20–21).

Christian philosopher Dallas Willard goes even further than Yancey by suggesting that the normative Christian experience enjoys an intimate and even conversational relationship with God/Jesus.[5] In Willard's view this highly personal interaction may occur in a variety of ways. First, through blind faith we may develop a strong conviction or perception that God is near, regardless of any supporting evidence. Secondly, we may be impressed that God is revealed through some circumstance—a worship service or some other event may trigger a sense of God's presence. Thirdly, events may transpire in our lives that can only be attributed to God. We receive news, for example, that a terminal disease miraculously vanished or that a hopelessly broken marriage was restored and become convinced that only God could have accomplished such a turn of fortune.

Willard acknowledges that all three of these ways of hearing God are highly subjective and may represent only "vague feelings" or "superstitious conjecture."[6] Yet, we would be hard pressed to deny the important role feelings have in life with God. Without feelings and sensations much of our spiritual life would be impoverished, if not eliminated. But when our feelings operate disconnected from the input and discernment of a wider faith community, there is the distinct possibility that the voice we hear is not God's but our own.

Willard concurs that these three ways of hearing God require support from more concrete sources. He offers two additional ways of hearing God that he says are more reliable: Scripture and the immersion of one's life into doing God's work. Willard believes these two sources place hearing God on more secure footing.

Willard writes that God most clearly speaks through Scripture. By reading the Bible and meditating upon what we read, we hear God "speaking preserved in written form."[7] In Willard's judgement the Bible provides believers with assurances that through the written word God can be heard.

His conviction that God speaks through the sacred writings has been embraced by people of faith searching for an authentic encounter with God for millennia. Over centuries these faith experiences were written down and became enshrined as reliable and faithful accounts of how people lived life with God. These written journals were deemed insightful spiritual guides and have stood the test of time, and by listening to Scripture we can eavesdrop on past generations of faith, as they struggled, debated, prayed, and grew in their understanding of God. They serve today as resources that provide wisdom and spiritual counsel to people looking for an authentic path to God.

Certainly, there is much to be gained from reading the Bible and attentively listening to Scripture. By dialoging with other people about the meaning of these writings, we may become more attuned to what it means to live a life of faith. Still, Scripture never represents itself as a means for direct, unmediated access to God. The Bible is a witness to how people experienced God, but it does not portray as normative an intimate and familiar relationship with God.

The Apostle Paul valued Scripture as a useful tool but did not attribute it as a way to know God directly (2 Tim. 3:15–17). While Jesus reveals God, the New Testament mediates Jesus. To take Yancey's phrase, the Bible is a "means of grace" that indirectly reveals God/Jesus to us.[8] As a means of grace, the biblical writings need to be interpreted, analyzed, prayed over, and debated in order to hear divine truth. In reading the Bible factors like culture, language, personal biases and prejudices, education, and a host of other issues need to be considered. Where God's voice is heard in Scripture the words are cloaked by these uniquely human factors. While providing an indispensable record of Israel's and the church's faith journey and their growing spiritual understanding, the Bible offers only a mediated or indirect experience with God. In order to hear God speak through Scripture, we must listen not only attentively but also collectively, because hearing the Word of God is not merely an acoustical function but involves the necessity of an open heart and a connection to the larger community of faith.

Willard's second more reliable way of hearing God is by immersing ourselves in God's work—caring for the sick, feeding the hungry, and other acts of kindness. Through a life of moral and ethical engagement we become sensitive to God's presence and approval.[9] As we serve God through selfless acts of compassion, God's Spirit may touch our lives and we may encounter divine presence.

During the course of my ministry I took a number of mission trips with church members. One year I traveled with twelve other men to a small village in Kyrgyzstan. For two weeks we worked on building a schoolhouse for Muslim children in the community. Every day we spent time with the villagers, played soccer with the children (who never failed to beat us), shared meals with the people and even attended a Muslim wedding, where I was asked to give a blessing to the couple. Throughout all these experiences we found that we had much in common with our Muslim friends. Even though we spoke different languages, worshipped differently and came from different cultures, we were human beings cut from the same divine image. It was an unforgettable time. When our plane landed back in the States we were all changed. Through offering and receiving acts of love in relationship with other people, we felt God's presence in refreshing ways that would mark our lives forever. Willard makes an important point: We become aware of God's presence through caring and unselfish acts of love.

You don't have to travel to a faraway place to sense the touch of God. Taking time to listen closely to a friend at work or buying lunch for a homeless person and then sitting down and eating with him or visiting a lonely woman in a care facility or other acts of love can draw us closer to God. The more we give of ourselves, the greater our awareness of the sacredness of all life, and affirming the sacredness of life places us within listening distance of God.

Willard's emphasis on Scripture and acts of love moves us closer to understanding how God draws near and can lead to a more hope-filled life. We need more than individual subjective feelings to live by, and Scripture and acts of love can construct a more solid foundation for life with God. Later, I will dive deeper into the role that Scripture and acts of love play in providing a foundation for hope, but first I want to examine a little more closely Willard's usage of the word "conversation," and Yancey's description of life with God as a "personal relationship."

The term conversation, aligned with the modern notion of how we understand a personal relationship, can be misleading and give the impression of a casual or even intimate familiarity with God. In a culture steeped in hyper-individualism, as ours is, promoting a direct and unmediated access to God as a "normative" Christian experience fails to capture an accurate biblical description of the life of faith. Perhaps Willard's stress on Scripture and acts of love illustrates what he means by "normative" conversation with God—indirect channels of grace that create an environment for us to experience God's presence. In other words, Willard may intend for us to understand conversation as mediated communication, mediated through the church, Bible, serving others in selfless acts of love, the sacraments, and any number of other channels of grace.

Through the years I have known people who claimed to have had conversations with God. Usually what they meant by conversation was not direct dialogue but rather a sense of God's presence and general leadership through the reading of the Bible and by following its teachings and by participating in community. Nevertheless, in today's narcissistic culture the concept of conversation suggests a familiarity with God that occurs with only a few people in all of Scripture. The writings of history tell us of terrible crimes against humanity perpetrated by those who professed intimate and direct access to God.[10]

If you and I feel as though God speaks directly and personally to us, we can easily be convinced that God is on our side. And, if God is on our side, other people can easily be dehumanized as God's enemies, thereby justifying our inhumane treatment of them. The mistreatment in our past of Native Americans and the racial discrimination against Black and Hispanic peoples as well as the denigration of Muslim immigrants come to mind as contemporary examples of how segments of the "Christian" population were supposedly in conversation with God. People's confidence that they enjoy an intimate dialogue with God and have unmediated access to him can justify in their minds brutal treatment of people deemed enemies of the faith.

Claims of a privileged intimacy with God tend to elevate some people while marginalizing others. To describe our experience with God as conversational confers a level of closeness that approaches spiritual arrogance. The clearest example is the special but misunderstood status that Israel had with God during the Davidic monarchy and the following generations that led to national disaster. Israel's mistaken belief that an elected people were not accountable to live a humane and godly lifestyle was condemned by the prophets throughout Scripture and causally resulted in the destruction of the temple and Israel's captivity.

That conversations with God are rare does not mean that God does not hear our prayers. As people of faith we pray and believe that God listens, but our prayers are not two-way conversations with God, at least not in the way that most of us would define conversation. Prayer diverts attention away from ourselves, a much needed corrective in our modern culture, and redirects our focus to the concerns of God. Jewish theologian Abraham Heschel acknowledges the importance of prayer by suggesting that prayer is our response to the goodness of creation and reflects our willingness to submit to do God's will on earth. Prayer opens our heart to God and brings to God's attention both our hopes and our regrets. Our goal in prayer, then, seeks not to know God but, more importantly, reveals our heart to God so that we may "be known to Him."[11]

Some of us might dismiss Heschel's views on prayer as representative of Jewish thought and irrelevant to Christian faith. Before we do that, however, consider the prayer that Jesus taught his disciples to pray and has served the church as a model prayer for the past 2,000 years (Matt. 6:9–13; Luke. 11:2–4). Although the church has claimed this prayer as its own, the prayer fits right in with Heschel's understanding. While a few Christian theologians have singled out Jesus' reference to God as Father as uniquely Christian, first century Jews also prayed to God as Father, and the remainder of the prayer follows a theological line of thought that finds support in either synagogue or church. Prayer, indeed, calls God's attention to our needs, but its primary purpose serves as a means for us to get on board with God and align our wills with God's will.

By praying for God's will to be done on earth, New Testament scholar Eugene Boring states that believers "cannot pray this prayer without committing [their] own will and action to fulfilling the will of God in the present and praying that other people will submit themselves to God's rule in the here and now."[12] When we pray "Our Father," we are not entering into a chummy little talk with God, but rather we are committing ourselves to participate in a family of faith that seeks to live out God's image in the world, that is, to be a people who "do what is right and good" (Gen. 18:19).[13]

Ironically, the phrase "personal relationship," so often used to describe what it means to live life with God, may actually drive us further away from divine presence by deceiving us into believing that we are closer to God than what we really are. Yancey correctly understands that a relationship with God is not equal to a relationship we have with each other. The idea of personal relationship implies a casual intimacy with God that artificially removes the mystery inherent in the divine/human encounter. While the Bible provides terms such as Father, Shepherd, Lover, Savior, these warm and personal attributes are best understood in a communal context, as analogies to human relationships that help us better visualize God as a being who deeply cares about us. Clearly, the individual has infinite worth before God, but the Bible emphasizes that God is most clearly known through community—through worship, hospitality, and other acts of kindness toward others.[14] Even when terms describe God's personal nature toward the individual, the broader community stands in close proximity. Church, assembly, congregation or community better frame how a relationship with God is pictured in the pages of Scripture.

One would think that an expression so highly popular in today's church culture would be scattered throughout Scripture, but that is not the case. Without a doubt there are numerous passages that signal God's love and commitment for individuals and nations. God is even described as "Father" in both Old and New Testaments. The personal nature of God is well attested to in the Bible but there is limited support for that relationship to be a familiar, casual or intimate one.

RETHINKING CONVERSATION AND PERSONAL RELATIONSHIP WITH GOD

How often the phrase "God told me" is uttered to win an argument or confirm a personal bias. If God and I are good buddies, then of course I must be right and you must be wrong. Such confident assertions do much damage both in and beyond the faith community. By claiming intimacy with God, the divine name is dragged down to the depths of human hubris, a direct violation of the commandment not to take the Lord's name in vain (Exod. 20:7). To take God's name in "vain" means to "take it lightly" or "casually" or "without thinking." Even sincere people of faith can be guilty of breaking this commandment by employing God's name for personal advantage.

Several years ago a woman came to see me who was concerned about her marriage. I listened while she told me about her dysfunctional relationship with her husband. From her vantage point, her husband was an uncaring, unloving, thoughtless, and self-centered man. She was tired of living with him but because their children were elementary age, she didn't feel she could divorce him.

I was not surprised when she finally admitted that she had been involved with another man for several months. "He is such a wonderful person," she shared with me. "He understands me, pays attention to my needs, and we love each other." Then she quickly added, "I know you probably think this is wrong, but *I have prayed about this matter, and God has told me that he knows how unhappy I have been and he wants me to be happy."*

The woman's perceived personal relationship with God gave her permission to break her marriage vows. Through her private conversations with God, apart from the community of faith, she sincerely believed that her affair had divine approval, a clear example of what it means to take God's name in vain.

We are frail and fallible creatures, and sometimes marriages fail. The woman was right to want a healthy marriage relationship, a partner with whom she could be happy. But did she have to invoke God's name to justify her decision to seek happiness outside her marriage? Would she blame God if her affair ended in disappointment and heartbreak? Her short-sighted behavior would probably result in pain for everyone.

Unfortunately, her misunderstanding of what it means to live life with God allowed her to believe that whatever she was thinking and feeling, God must also be thinking and feeling. In this instance God became a reflection of herself. And by not recognizing her own culpability in her unhappy marriage, she was denying herself the experience of being able to fully appreciate the magnitude of God's grace. The confession of a hopelessly broken marriage could have served as a sign of repentance, provided a new beginning and allowed God's grace to heal both her husband's and her damaged lives. The marriage may have ended, but their integrity as human beings created in the image of God did not have to. But if grace is taken for granted as a right, something we deserve, then it ceases to be God's gift. When we view grace in this way, our spiritual growth is stunted. For whenever we alone make up our own set of rules in matters of faith, we will ultimately lose our way.

Throughout my ministry a number of people confided in me that God, if not condoning unethical or immoral behavior, at least looked the other way. Convinced that God was their best friend, they felt that God/Jesus would surely understand their situation and grant them a longer moral leash. To believe that God and I are on a conversational basis and have a personal and intimate relationship can result in thinking that life with God grants me special privileges to bend or even break the rules.

When we habitually define our experience with God in exclusive terms as a private encounter apart from the larger community of faith, we can readily come to believe our thoughts are God's thoughts and our ways, God's ways. To believe that God cares about me and listens to my prayer is one thing. To further believe that I can push aside the mystery encompassing life with God and directly encounter God on my terms is quite another thing. There is biblical support for the first belief. The second belief is a product of the modern age with its extreme emphasis on the individual self. This modern belief does not reflect the experiences of the men and women of Scripture. A community can steady our understanding of life with God by helping us to focus beyond our own desires to the needs of those around us—a positive sign that we are on an authentic journey of faith.

We see through a mirror darkly, and because our vision is limited there is never room for arrogance or pride. Divine mystery removes any pretense that I can know God's mind better than you. If we are fortunate enough to enjoy a blessed life, it is human nature to delude ourselves into thinking that we have earned intimacy with God. It is then natural to believe that those poor souls suffering through the darker and colder currents of faith must have done something to merit God's displeasure. Nothing could be further from the truth. The various stages of faith often have little to do with our standing before God. Too many times I have spent my mornings with a sense of God's closeness, only to climb into my car at the end of the workday and feel as though God had completely abandoned me. I have learned that my fickle human nature shoulders much of the blame for my feelings of spiritual insecurity.

Community, Scripture, and acts of love can stabilize feelings of emotional whiplash. These and other means of grace can pour a more secure foundation for life with God that can better prepare us for life's unpredictable turns. The importance of community, however, cannot be overstated. After all, it takes a community to hear the word of God, and, still, the community must pray, debate, contemplate, and sometimes wring its hands in exasperation in an effort to discern God's word. Even then the community does not have the last word, for when we think we have heard God, we must keep listening. For tomorrow God may open our minds and hearts a little more, and we may learn that what we thought we knew was only the beginning.

CHAPTER 7

THE GOD WHO PLAYS HIDE & SEEK

Truly, you are a God who hides.

- Isaiah

As a pastor I had to guard against taking myself too seriously. Congregations have a tendency to place pastors on pedestals, and, what's even worse, sometimes we pastors have a tendency to think we belong there.

One summer Sunday morning after church I walked to my car feeling pretty good about myself. The sermon had gone well and a number of members were rather generous in their praise of my homiletical skills. I stopped in front of my car, which I always parked under a large oak tree, and began to take off my coat. When I opened the car door the birds in the tree overhead were apparently spooked by the sound of the door opening and took off by the dozens, not before, however, depositing their morning breakfast on me. Well, on second thought, maybe my most discerning listener wasn't so impressed with my sermon!

God does have a way of communicating with us in strange and mysterious ways. With Jacob, God spoke through a dream; with Isaiah, it was a vision; with Job, God spoke out of a whirlwind. The Bible describes God as a person, but God's personal nature is mysterious and elusive. Encounters with God do take place in Scripture, but these moments are rare and even when they do occur, God's presence is experienced only partially—enough to awaken our God-consciousness but never enough for us to take God's presence for granted. In Scripture people usually experienced God in subtle ways—they heard a strange sound, or they encountered a mysterious natural wonder or they entertained a strange guest. Encounters with God are filled with ambiguity, trepidation, and uncertainty. An experience with God is normally associated with fear, awe, dread, profound reverence and mystery, and maybe from time to time a few bird droppings.[1]

A number of years ago over lunch a young banker explained to me that he didn't believe there was anything mysterious about God. At first I thought he was setting me up for a punch line to some joke, a bit of humor to put my rather sober demeanor at ease. But he was serious. "Sometimes," he continued, "Christians think we are part of some great mystery. I don't believe that. God has made himself known through Jesus and the Bible tells us in black and white language everything we need to know about God. There is nothing complicated about faith."

I swallowed my hardly chewed enchilada, almost choking on it, thinking how I could answer him without ruining both of our lunches. Driving back to the church several hours later I replayed our conversation. The young man was a successful commercial banker and was active in our congregation. He taught a class of high school boys and was popular with the group. I deeply cared about him and his family. My first reaction was anger at myself. How could I have failed not to have conveyed to him the hallmark of biblical faith—the elusive and mysterious nature of God?

There is a segment within the church that feels threatened by too much wiggle room in matters relating to faith. The purpose of religion, according to these believers, is certainty and assurance. From their religious perspective, faith in God is not intended to cast doubt or create anxiety. After all, they reason, God is not the author of confusion. If the primary goal of their religion is to shield them from existential anxieties, then it makes sense for these people to reject a religious view that embraces mystery and uncertainty in their relationship with God.

The Bible, however, does not depict life with God without mystery. From the first pages of Scripture to the last, faith and mystery are intertwined. While there are many passages in Scripture that underscore this perspective, the creation story of Adam and Eve is a good place to start. In this Edenic paradise we gain insight into how human beings in their innocence first encountered God.

IN THE GARDEN

The Genesis creation story reaches its climax when "God created humankind in his image, in the image of God he created them; male and female he created them" (Gen. 1:27 NRSV). The opening chapter of the Bible announces that in some mysterious way both man and woman have been chiseled from the divine block. It is a stunning concept and signifies the intrinsic value and universal dignity of human life. We people of flesh and blood contain within us the stuff of our Creator.

Theologians have long speculated about just exactly how we are "created in the image of God" but there has been no consensus. One proposal suggests that our ability to engage with others on a personal level differentiates us from the rest of the animal world and identifies us with God. That we can love and interact with other individuals and risk our lives on their behalf are qualities we may share with God. To think and reason on an abstract level may connect us with our Maker as well. However we are related to God, one thing is clear: All human life is precious beyond calculation because we in some unique way bear within us something of our Creator.

The psalmist, in a moment of gleeful delight, captures the majesty of human life by effusively proclaiming that human beings have been created only "a little lower than the divine" (Ps. 8:5)[1]. High praise, indeed, for creatures made from the dirt of the earth. From the moment God breathed divine spirit into our nostrils—the breath of life—we were intended to represent God's presence on earth. Our role is "to keep" or "take care of" or "protect" the home we have been given (Gen. 2:15).

While there are many possible avenues of intrigue to pursue in the creation story, the one that piques my curiosity is how the biblical writers describe the relationship between God and the Creator's first human creatures. If ever the divine/human experience were to exhibit personal warmth and an uninhibited exchange of thoughts, this would be the time. In their state of complete innocence the first couple would no doubt enjoy a close and intimate relationship with God. Adam and Eve were free of sin, without moral failure, and eager to enter into relationship with God. But did they?

We might think, for instance, that after the creation of Adam, he and God would have enjoyed intimate companionship, much like the special bond that a father and son enjoy. It seems strange, therefore, that the biblical writers leave the impression of a rather ambiguous interaction between the two. In fact, the Bible reveals a relationship between God and Adam that lacks personal and direct intimacy. It is as if the father brings his son into the world, and then, after a what-not-to-do lecture, waves him off to fend for himself. There is no indication from Scripture of ongoing warm and personal interactions.

For sure God's love and compassion for the man can be seen in the moment of Adam's creation, when God breathed life into the man, an incredibly vivid portrayal of the unique spiritual connection man has with God. But God's presence remains strangely elusive. Adam experiences only fleeting encounters with God, encounters that leave the man unfulfilled and lonely. The man enjoyed and shared life not with God, but instead with the other creatures—the animals. These lowly creatures, however, can't satisfy man's need for companionship and fulfillment.

The story paints a rather dismal picture of Adam's life in Paradise. Seemingly, he has everything, but in truth, he has almost nothing. Even in a perfect world, without a personal relationship, his life lacks meaning and completeness. Who is there to talk to, to laugh with, to take walks with, to watch a sun set with or to love. There is no one with whom he can share his life or be intimate. Adam lives in a garden paradise, except that it isn't. Without human love it is a beautiful but lonely place. I wonder if Adam's loneliness didn't result in a form of depression. After all, he is human and a perpetually isolated human being can grow weary with life.

Why hasn't God taken notice of Adam's emotional pain, his need for companionship, and sought to comfort him? Why hasn't God taken a stroll through the garden, sat down with the distraught man and listened attentively to his forlorn son? Any kind of communication would have been welcomed; any sign of personal warmth would surely have eased Adam's unbearable emptiness. Yes, we the reader see signs of God's love for Adam in every act of creation, but human beings need more than things. Human beings cannot survive without relationships, and, for whatever reason, God chooses not to directly engage with Adam.

Clearly, God makes every provision to keep Adam alive. A garden provides food and nourishment. All of Adam's physical needs are met. Yet

Adam appears miserable and even God acknowledges as much, "It is not good that the man should be alone. I will make him a helper as his partner" (Gen. 2:18 NRSV). There is no misery worse than waking up day after day totally alone, and Adam is alone. Whatever relationship Adam had with God, it didn't provide the kind of fulfillment he needed.

At last, when enough time has elapsed for Adam to name all the animals, God acts and shows concern and compassion for Adam but without directly engaging on a personal level. Instead, God creates another human being man can relate to. Using architectural vocabulary, the Bible tells us God "fashions" or "builds" a woman from the side of man. There is no indication the patient had a pre- or post-op consultation with his divine surgeon. In all likelihood Adam was clueless as to God's plan. When he awakens, God plays the role of matchmaker and introduces Adam to his partner, Eve, but then God once again slides into the background. It is Eve who is to be man's "helper," a word that implies "succor" or "support" or even "to save." It is woman who saves man, and it is woman who will become the man's companion, his soulmate. The rib taken from the side of man symbolizes the woman's co-equal status, together they will serve as partners in caring for the earth.

God elects to send a human being to rescue Adam from what would have been a life of despair. Even in Paradise all is not perfect until woman brings to man what he needs most—an intimate, personal relationship. Only in relationship with another human being was the design of creation complete.

Whatever passed between God and Adam in the garden in those first moments of human existence, it never rose to the level of a warm, personal and familiar bond. In a world void of other human beings Adam's experience with God was not sufficient to relieve him of his deeply felt need for something more. Only another human being, someone like himself, could assuage that cavernous emptiness.

The Genesis storytellers continue to show that the relationship between God and God's human creatures remains formal and indirect. After their act of disobedience, the couple hear God stirring in the garden in the cool of the day (Gen. 3:8), although they do not see God directly. They only hear a voice, or as the Hebrew cryptically suggests—a sound, but they do not directly observe God. Adam and Eve sense God's presence and are aware that God knows of their disobedience, but they do not seek out God. Instead, they hide. Why are they afraid? Does fear define their relationship with God more than love? Are they more familiar with God's indifference than they are of God's compassion?

God calls out to them. Adam answers. God speaks to them and words are exchanged, but God's self is never unambiguously revealed. God's accessibility remains distant and hidden. Information passes between them, but the couple's response further betrays not only their flawed character but also their estranged relationship with God.

To be sure, there are elements of the personal in the garden story, but the encounter does not meet the standard of what most of us would consider a personal relationship. An encounter, yes; a personal relationship, no. The scene reeks with tension and unease, and with each syllable that God speaks the chasm appears to grow wider. Adam and Eve do not prolong the exchange or seriously engage in conversation with God. Their only spoken words are defensive in nature—they make excuses for their act of disobedience. What has always been a rather elusive connection now becomes an obviously strained and distant one.

The garden story teases the reader with the hope that God and the first couple will somehow move past their fumbling efforts at establishing a relationship, but it never quite gets there. We desperately desire to see God, Adam and Eve sitting down together, eating, laughing and enjoying one another's company. All the trappings are there for such a moment before their ruinous act—a garden paradise, innocent children and all the time in the universe. The story is so tantalizingly close to what we all long for—a direct and personal relationship with God. But what the Genesis narrative portrays is a missed opportunity.

Even after their disobedience there is still the possibility of repentance and restoration, but it seems as though Adam and Eve do not trust God. Their prior experiences with God, even in their state of innocence, have not given them the confidence needed to approach their Creator. The verbal back-and-forth between God and the couple conveys raw facts, but not the sharing of selves, which is characteristic of intimate communication. The couple equivocate with God and pass the buck. Meaningful conversation requires transparency and the willingness to be vulnerable; otherwise the words represent mere chatter. For meaningful dialogue to take place on a personal level, participants must share an obligation for truth-telling, which reveals mutual respect. In contrast, Adam and Eve experience God only as an object who they try to manipulate and deceive, not as a valued conversational partner.

The lack of an engaging personal relationship falls not just on the shoulders of the first couple. God bears responsibility, too. Throughout the narrative there remains an unbridgeable divide between the two parties. God chooses not to make divine presence directly accessible but relates to the couple indirectly, creating additional space for misunderstanding, making a personal relationship an unlikely event. God, while clearly the focal point throughout the story, is also, paradoxically, a hidden and inaccessible figure.

In the beginning of the human story the Bible underscores the mystery associated with God. Adam lived in a world not yet stained by sin, but his experience with God could not fill the emotional emptiness within him. The man lived in a paradise that would ultimately have been a hell on earth, a place without companionship and intimacy. Only Eve's presence provided the human touch that saved Adam from a life of incompleteness and futility. Only in relationship with another human being did hope become more than wishful fantasy.

This early biblical story reveals the divide between God and Adam that is only further highlighted when God entered the garden. There is a sense God does not know where the man is. God questions, "Where are you?" (Gen. 3:9 NRSV). Perhaps it is only a greeting or maybe the phrase is only rhetorical. Regardless, there is an implied distance between God and the man. Earlier God had affirmed Adam's loneliness and now the evasive nature of God is writ large—God cannot or chooses not to make divine presence fully accessible to Adam. To experience companionship Adam had to look elsewhere, to another human being.

MYSTERY IN PATRIARCHAL FAITH

I first started reading the Bible when I was a teenager. The Bible stories fascinated me, especially the ones in the Old Testament. People like Abraham, Moses and others seemed bigger than life, like super heroes. It seemed to me that they enjoyed direct, even intimate conversations with God. I thought how cool it would be if God spoke to me that way. If God communicated with me the way God did with the patriarchs of old, there wouldn't be the need for faith; we would have certainty and life would be a whole lot easier or so it seemed.

It is fairly typical for Christians to think that during biblical times people routinely engaged directly with God. Biblical figures such as Abraham and Moses, it is assumed, experienced God in less enigmatic ways than we do today. Modern readers of the Bible are sometimes inclined to believe that in ancient times God pulled the curtain back and allowed these heroic patriarchs to experience unmediated divine presence. Consequently, there would have been no room for doubt or uncertainty in their relationship. These biblical giants lived on a mountaintop of faith, not in a ceaseless whirlpool of doubt. In other words, people in the Bible experienced God radically different from what we do today. But did they really?

Did people like Abraham and Moses experience God with more objective certainty than modern believers? Did they have an advantage over us? Did they have less reason to doubt? Was faith easier for them than it is for us? By reading closely a sampling of scriptural stories we may gain a better understanding of how our biblical forbears lived life with God.

Abraham and the Three Visitors (Gen. 18: 1-16)

The story of Abraham and the three divine visitors is one of my favorites in the Bible. By reading the text closely and understanding the historical background, we can gather a better sense of whether our present-day experiences are different from those of our biblical ancestors.

The story begins in verse one by informing the reader that God "appeared" to Abraham. At first glance we might assume that Abraham was completely aware that he was being visited by divine presence, but the first verse is for the benefit of the reader. It serves as a kind of preface to the rest of the story.

Abraham's story begins with verse two when the three strangers unexpectedly arrived. As the story unfolds, it becomes clear that he didn't know the identity of his guests. Epiphanies typically occurred suddenly and without warning in the Bible as God had a way of catching people off guard. So, true to form, divine presence entered into Abraham's life when he least expected it. While we, the reader, know that the strangers were divine personages, Abraham did not.

The guests appeared tired, hungry and thirsty, which would have been understandable for travelers in that part of the world. If God's intention was to unambiguously reveal divine presence, why the subterfuge? Why the pretense of needing rest and refreshment? The men looked and acted like ordinary human beings and Abraham had no reason to be suspicious.

Part of the genius of the story is how it captivates the audience. The audience knows from the opening verse that Abraham was being visited by God. Our knowledge and Abraham's lack of creates an intriguing situation, as we listen to Abraham treat God with no more nor no less respect than any ordinary stranger. If Abraham had known from the beginning that these strangers were of divine origin, why did he act so completely normal, as if the entire encounter were routine, something he did from time to time. I find myself completely engaged and attentive as the story proceeds, for I know what Abraham doesn't.

Abraham, of course, did what any respectable host would do. He invited the strangers to stay for lunch. It would have been rude not to. In the ancient world, to turn away guests was not only disrespectful, it was dangerous. There were no fast food restaurants or gas stations every few miles, and to ignore the common courtesies of hospitality might have resulted in someone's death. There was nothing about Abraham's actions that indicate he knew his guests' identities. He did what any gracious host would have done.

The entire episode is ensconced in subtleties. The three visitors rested under a tree, a completely normal action given the noonday heat, while Abraham had a meal prepared. He instructed Sarah to bake some bread and ordered servants to kill a tender calf. Abraham even provided fresh milk. Everything was brought to the guests and "they ate." It appears to be a perfectly normal act of neighborliness, something Abraham must have done many times before.

From the bowing to the serving of bread, meat and drink to the verbal exchange, the reader is privy to a secret of which Abraham was unaware. Abraham didn't have a clue that he was having burgers and a shake with the Almighty! It is this very experience of entertaining God unaware that gives the story its power: In the common and routine affairs of life we may unknowingly encounter divine presence. Biblical scholar Gerhard von Rad comments on this passage that "the narrative preserves a veil of mystery by allowing none of the persons [divine persons] to speak an actual identifying statement."[2] Abraham was surrounded by divine presence and didn't even know. But the reader knows and is warned to be on guard. God's mysterious presence may slip into our world unannounced, cloaked in the guise of common humanity!

God appeared to Abraham incognito, as apparently is God's way. When did Abraham finally realize who his visitors were? The text does not make that clear, but later in verse 14 Abraham's God-consciousness may have been somewhat awakened because he says, "Is anything too wonderful for the LORD?" The question is pregnant with sacred implications. The Hebrew word used here for LORD is YHWH, God's mysterious and unpronounceable name, itself a mystery but also a telling signal that Abraham knew he was in the presence of the Holy. Moreover, the word "wonderful" refers to something extraordinary, another clue that Abraham realized he stood before holy presence. But, then again, maybe Abraham never really knew for sure, but had only a sense that he had been a recipient of a divine visitation?

What fascinates me about this story is that it remarkably preserves the element of faith in Abraham's encounter with God. God did not overwhelm this nomadic rancher and shepherd. God seldom works that way. Divine presence is rarely announced with trumpets heralding the Almighty and angelic hosts singing the Hallelujah chorus. The renowned teacher and preacher Fred Craddock often said that to perceive God's presence requires us to lean over as far as we can and listen very closely. If we're not paying attention, we may miss out.

The New Testament further underscores the elusive nature of divine presence. Even the human presence of Jesus was not self-evident as God-in-the-flesh. Divine presence in Jesus was not so transparent that anyone could see him and say, "Well, I declare, that's the Son of God." Some people thought Jesus was a drunkard, and some within his own family thought he was mentally missing a marble or two. For three years the disciples followed Jesus, listened to him teach, watched him perform miracle after miracle, spoke with him in private about an assortment of issues, but after three years did they really know who Jesus was? When Jesus asked them point-blank, they said he might be John the Baptist or maybe Elijah or Jeremiah or even some other prophet (Matt. 16:13–20). Only Peter ventured to suggest that Jesus was Messiah. But even that confession lacked understanding, as evidenced by Peter's later betrayal. The disciples continued to struggle with both belief and doubt even after the resurrection. In the presence of the risen Jesus Matthew tells us that the disciples both worshipped him and doubted (Matt. 28:17).

And we are to believe that Abraham discerned God's identity among three ordinary looking strangers over lunch? Maybe the shadow receded for Abraham much in the same way it does for us—slowly. Over time, through prayer and reflection, we may grow to an awareness that God, perhaps through some completely everyday and mundane activity, slipped into our lives.

The story of Abraham and the three lunch guests evinces the elusive nature of God's presence. The episode is replete in earthiness and shrouded in mystery. While there is an element of the personal in Abraham's encounter with the strangers, it would be a stretch to describe what took place on that hot afternoon as an open and transparent personal relationship. It is as though Abraham was in a fog. When the three divine personages finally departed, Abraham's mind was probably dizzy with speculation, wondering what had just happened. The experience had a surreal quality that comes across in the pages of Scripture. Abraham, too, must have been tempted to have relegated the episode to the world of dreams. But the experience stayed with him. He never forgot it; that is why the story was preserved in Scripture for all of us to cherish. Be attentive! We, too, may entertain divine presence unaware. How I would have loved to have eavesdropped on the dinner conversation between Abraham and Sarah later that evening.

The Test (Gen. 22:1–19)

One of the most horrific stories found in Scripture takes place when God instructs Abraham to sacrifice his son, Isaac, as a burnt offering. Abraham hears only a voice. We know that God is testing Abraham, but Abraham doesn't know it's a test. He obediently prepares to offer his precious son as an offering to God. Isaac knows nothing of his impending death.

When Abraham and his son reach the location for the sacrifice, the father ties his son to the altar and raises his knife to do the unspeakable deed. Only then does Abraham hear from heaven. But the voice he hears is not God's but an angel's. It is almost as if God is embarrassed to have put such a hideous thought in Abraham's mind. The son is spared. The Old Testament scholar Samuel Terrien writes that with Isaac's deliverance the reliability of God was preserved, "Intimacy between God and Israel is secure."[3] Intimacy secure? I respectfully disagree. How can such a request insure intimacy between God and his people? Granted, Abraham did not kill his son, but that God would even lead Abraham to contemplate such an evil would forever decimate his confidence in God. In the back of Abraham's mind he would always wonder, "Can I trust this God?" Traumatic experiences are not soon forgotten. Abraham didn't forget. As far as we know, he never spoke to God again. Who can blame him?

And how would Abraham's son ever be able to put this nightmare behind him? Soren Kierkegaard recognizes the psychological damage that would have hung around the boy's neck from that day forward. If he were to think that God instructed his death on the altar, how could Isaac ever trust God? How could there be intimacy with God after that experience? In Kierkegaard's insightful interpretation, Abraham wants to shield his son from thinking anything negative about God. To spare Isaac from believing that God would ask such a thing, Abraham assumes the role of the murderer. Kierkegaard puts words in father Abraham's mouth, "Do you think it is God's command? No, it is my desire. Then Isaac trembled and cried out in his anguish: 'God in heaven, have mercy on me; if I have no father on earth then you be my father!' But Abraham said softly to himself, 'Lord God in heaven, I thank you; it is better that he believes me a monster than that he should lose faith in you.'"[4]

The story offends our moral sense of right and wrong. How could God ask such a thing? The point of the story, of course, is that Abraham demonstrated his willingness to obey God, regardless of the cost, and, therefore, is forever remembered as a man of faith. In what way God revealed divine presence to Abraham is left to the imagination. What is clear, however, is that Abraham had no assured certainty how the story would end.

There are many experiences in the Book of Genesis between God and Abraham. But when closely examined these encounters usually fall far short of an objective experience with God. As we read earlier, not long after Abraham had sensed God's call (Gen. 15), he still had to exercise faith, and even then his encounters with God could always be second-guessed. On the front end of these experiences I don't think Abraham had any more assurance than we do today. Following God was as challenging for him as it is for people in the so-called modern world. Doing what was right was as difficult for him as it is for us. Throughout the many divine/human interactions with Abraham God stays in character by not revealing divine presence in direct and unambiguous ways. God's nature remains elusive.

Moses and the Burning Bush (Exod. 3:1-4:17)

Many of us have seen Hollywood's version of the Ten Commandments. Moses, played by Charlton Heston, climbs Mount Sinai and stands before a burning bush and audibly hears the voice of God. The voice tells Moses that he will be God's instrument to liberate the enslaved Israelites. Usually around Easter the movie reappears on television, and I invariably find myself watching it. Unfortunately, Cecil B. DeMille's rendering of the historic event may be more theater than Scripture.

The entire movie has an out-of-this-world quality to it. To have been confronted by God in such a straightforward way, as the cinematic drama suggests, would have left little room for Moses to exercise faith. It would have completely overwhelmed him. That makes for great entertainment, but I doubt if Moses had such a melodramatic epiphany. In Scripture God seldom overpowers the recipients of divine presence to the point that the experience loses its subjectivity, a necessary component for faith.

Why does Moses hesitate after God speaks to him by making one excuse after another? He dodges God again and again with such excuses as: I'm not an eloquent speaker; I'm not an adequate leader; who am I to lead the people out of captivity? He gives God a number of reasons why he is not the right person for the job. Was Moses, like Abraham, unsure of what his heart and mind were telling him? Maybe he thought he was dreaming. Maybe he didn't trust his senses. Is the text giving us only the remembrance of the experience, a remembrance colored by faith? Hindsight may have recollected the event to Moses with much greater clarity than the actual happening.

The occurrence in real time, if video camera had been present, may have looked and sounded quite different. Whatever Moses saw and heard, there must have been wiggle room for alternate interpretations. The experience at Sinai did not give Moses irrefutable proof that he was in divine presence. Absent faith Moses may have completely missed this momentous event. After all, Pharaoh saw the same wonders of God but assigned to them a completely different explanation.

Even after all his excuses had been addressed by God, Moses' faith still exudes skepticism and suspicion. Finally, when he has run out of responses, he asks for the name of this God who speaks from the burning bush. God responds, "I am who I am" (Exod. 3:14 NRSV), an answer that clarifies nothing for Moses. The phrase "I am who I am" has been variously translated as "I am being that I am being" or "I will be all that you need me to be" or "I will cause to be what I will cause to be." Karen Armstrong renders the phrase with deliberate vagueness, "Never mind who I am."[5] She understands the difficult phrase to be an idiomatic expression comparing it to "They went where they went," meaning "I have no idea where they went." Moses wants answers; what he gets is more uncertainty and confusion.

Moses had a life-changing experience in his encounter with God on Sinai, but the experience left Moses with many unanswered questions. Even the name of God was couched in mystery. Still, Moses took a risk and set out for Egypt. His heart was conflicted; he was not without doubt, but I have learned that even an unsettled heart does not disqualify us from following God. If we wait to have all our questions answered before we venture out in faith, the ship will sail long before we board!

THE SHADOW RECEDES—SOMEWHAT (Exodus 33:7-11)

One of the more remarkable passages in Scripture is found in Exodus 33. In the previous chapter (Exod. 32) Israel had jeopardized her relationship with God by worshipping a golden calf. We might think that after witnessing the signs and wonders of God, Israel would have forever remained faithful. But that was not the case, and God's patience was growing thin. Israel, on the other hand, was promised a land flowing with milk and honey but found themselves in a barren wasteland. If God was losing patience with Israel, it didn't take long for Israel to lose patience with God. A prolonged and inhospitable wilderness can drain the life out of anyone, spiritually or physically.

I think many of us know the feeling. More times than I can count I have grown exasperated with God. Who among us has not prayed fervently for a sick child's recovery or an aged parent struggling with a terminal disease to die peacefully, only to have our prayers seemingly fall on deaf ears?

If Israel's faithfulness had much to be desired, I understand. The beleaguered people were no different than many of us. Still, if God had abandoned Israel, the nation would have lost its purpose for existence, and it would have been thrown into an endless season of despair. Plus, God would have lost a potentially valuable witness in Israel. Fortunately, Moses knew that and was eager to get God's attention and convince God that these unremarkable people were worth saving.

While Israel camped, still smarting from their outrageous act of idolatry, a tent of meeting was erected. The tent was outside the camp, probably on a hill where all the people could see what might possibly take place. The purpose of the tent of meeting was for God and the people to have a place where they could meet, ostensibly to iron out any problems that might arise. Although theoretically anyone was permitted to enter the tent, there is no indication that anyone other than Moses did so. Joshua was near or even in the tent, but he did not speak with God, nor is there any hint he was privy to the conversation.

It seems that Moses was the only one who met with God. When Moses entered the tent a cloud descended that mysteriously conveyed the presence of the Holy. The inference from the text indicates that the cloud both revealed and concealed God's presence. The visible earthiness of the cloud gave a kind of substance to God's visitation, but it also served to shield divine presence from human observation.

Within the place of meeting Moses spoke "face to face" with God "as a man speaks to a friend" (Exod. 33:11 NRSV). The implied intimacy between Moses and God is breathtaking and one of the most personal divine/human encounters in Scripture. Moreover, it was not a singular event, as later chapters suggest these conferences took place on a regular basis. Another striking feature about this passage is that God knew Moses by name, a rare occurrence in the Old Testament and a detail that adds warmth to the drama (Exod. 33:17).

If Exodus 33:12-23 reflects the type of conversations God and Moses had with each other, then the dialogue was not only intimate but also bold on Moses' part. Moses pushed God to pledge continued protective care for Israel, an Israel that God had only recently called a stiff-necked people. Considering that God had been ready to light a match to the entire nation (Exod. 33:3), Moses had quite a marketing strategy to figure out. But Moses did not back down and finally convinced God to stay the course with these obstinate people.

The perceived closeness Moses experienced with God gave him the temerity to ask God for a personal favor. Show me your "glory," Moses pleads. "Glory" refers to all that God is, God's complete self, God's majesty and grandeur. Moses wanted to know God fully, which would have opened the door to a new kind of human/divine relationship, one where the cloud no longer stood between Creator and creation.

But Moses had gone too far and that request would only be partially granted. While Moses enjoyed immediacy with God that few people in the Bible experienced, there was a limit to God's self-disclosure. Although God was not completely revealed to Moses, God did give Moses a brief glimpse of divine goodness or divine generosity. As God moved past the protected Moses, the curious prophet witnessed only the back side of God, a rather humorous descriptive euphemism (Exod. 33:21-23)! What limited divine presence Moses saw reassured him that God would continue to be attentive to the people of Israel.

The Bible indicates that for a period of time Moses enjoyed an unusually close relationship with God that, if not personal, was one of the most direct and unmediated divine encounters found in Scripture. Still, divine presence was never fully revealed to Moses. Within this unique divine/human relationship an impenetrable haze separated the two, preventing Moses from experiencing unimpeded access to God. Instead, God's elusive and mysterious nature yielded to Moses only a fleeting glance of God's posterior. The shadow receded but not completely.

Scholars have questioned whether parts of this story are out of place and for good reason.[6] There appears to be an element of inconsistency throughout the narrative. How can we square these unusual person to person meetings, which the Bible describes as a dialogue between two friends, with the hovering cloud that conveys distance and concealment? Then, too, Moses supposedly engaged with God in "face to face" personal conversations, which also adds an element of rapport to the story, yet a few verses later the text specifically warns: No person may see God and live (Exod. 33:20), which significantly modifies that perceived intimacy.

What are we to make of these apparent contradictions? On the one hand, the Bible seemingly tells us, "Yes, Moses knew God up close and personal," but then quickly reverses course and acknowledges, "No, Moses knew God only from a distance." Which is it? Is the Bible attempting a little theological sleight of hand? I don't think so. To the contrary, I believe the Bible is faithfully bearing witness to the mystery of a divine encounter where all the dots are never completely connected.

The lack of cohesiveness in the story illustrates the inscrutable ways of divine presence that transcend human comprehension. Human beings cannot fully grasp God's self-disclosure nor can divine presence be logically explained by the most gifted of writers. If Moses authored the Book of Exodus, as some scholars believe, then the narrative's inconsistencies suggest that even an eye witness account to a divine epiphany cannot capture the magnitude of the event. Whenever divine presence is encountered, there will always be gaps in the experience that can only be filled in by faith.

The discrepancies in the story do not trouble me. I would be more disturbed if every line harmonized, if all the i's were dotted and t's crossed. Then I would assume that later editors had meddled with the narrative to smooth off all the rough edges. The story as it now stands has greater plausibility, and the uneven structure has a reassuring quality that suggests an encounter with God is beyond the vocabulary of even inspired writers.

There is much to take away from this unique story. But what cannot be ignored is the elusive nature of God. Regardless of how sunny our faith disposition or how close we may think our relationship with God is, a shadow stands between divine presence and us. Some people are simply more aware of that shadow than others. Centuries ago an anonymous author recognized that all authentic faith walks with God more in the fog than in the light.[7] As much as we resist the thought, God's elusive and mysterious nature will forever mark the life of faith.

It would be fascinating to speak with Moses about his conversations with God. I have a truck load of questions I would like to ask him. After his meetings with God did he ever doubt again? Did he ever wrestle with the trustworthiness of God? I think he probably did. After all, he was human and humans have an insatiable appetite for certainty, to know completely. Moreover, no matter how many experiences of divine presence we may enjoy, the intrusion of an unexpected shadow has a way of blotting out all of our previous memories. Uncertainty will always be part of the equation of faith. To want more certainty in our life with God is human; to trust without it defines authentic faith.

Centuries later, three disciples, Peter, James and John, would see Jesus transfigured, where "his face shone like the sun, and his clothes became dazzling white." Both Moses and Elijah appeared with him (Matt. 17:2-3 NRSV). It was a stunning display of divine presence, and one would think that after such a spectacular event any trace of doubt would forever be put to rest. Not so. It wouldn't be long before these same disciples would fall asleep when Jesus desperately needed their support, and then they would abandon him when their lives were endangered. Regardless of the brightness of divine presence, our human nature prevents us from seeing clearly. When it comes to feeling secure in our life with God, there is never enough proof. No matter how often or how transparently God may enter into our lives, we always crave for more. I think Moses did too.

While Moses experienced an unusually personal relationship with God, divine presence was not completely revealed to Moses. Moses still had to exercise faith. Absolute certainty in his relationship with God remained out of reach. Samuel Terrien, a noted and respected biblical scholar, points out that in the "fifteen centuries [of the biblical period] the recurrent motif of divine nearness is historically limited to a few men. The sense of presence is persistently compounded with an awareness of absence."[8] Like so many of us, biblical figures knew a variety of faith stages, experiencing God's presence as well as divine absence. God's elusive nature precludes getting too comfortable with God. Even when God is present, divine presence remains cloaked in mystery.

CHAPTER 8

A MARINE CORPS INSTRUCTOR AND GOD

In every You we address the eternal You.

- Martin Buber

God's elusive and mysterious nature does not mean that we are left completely in the dark, unable to perceive divine presence in our lives. God leaves traces of divine presence in acts of love, Scripture and community, ways by which God reaches out and touches us, if only we exercise faith to receive these gifts. These "means of grace," while not direct and unmediated encounters with God and certainly not as revealing as we would like, nevertheless have the power to draw us closer to divine presence.

We might wonder, "How can we even know if we encounter divine presence?" We may think, "Surely, if God visits us, we would be aware. We would feel or sense a spiritual presence." I'm not so sure. Divine presence may quietly slip into our lives completely unobserved or unfelt, and if we have predetermined how the Holy must enter, say through some supernatural epiphany or touchy-feely experience, we may miss completely the wondrous event. God may enter into our lives in surprising and barely perceptible ways.

My introduction to the United States Marine Corps began the moment I stepped off the plane in Washington, D.C., and met my platoon sergeant. For the next twelve weeks this beast of a man would do his best to shape me and the other 200 or so candidates into something like Marine Corps officers. He was the most intimidating human being I have ever known. He had served two tours of duty in Vietnam and had been decorated for bravery. He demanded maximum effort in every exercise, drill and class period. He showed no mercy if a Marine dropped out of a training run due to fatigue and would dog stragglers relentlessly until they could keep up. During the first six weeks I was convinced that if I keeled over dead, he would have just picked up my carcass and thrown it into the nearest trash bin. I felt I was garbage to him. Then one day my attitude changed.

I had been coughing and sneezing for several days in the classroom, during physical training and especially at night in the squad bay. The platoon sergeant continually yelled at me to shut up, commenting harshly that they weren't running a tuberculous ward. Finally, he called me into his office and told me to report to sick bay. I thought, "He doesn't care about me. He only wants to get rid of me."

Later that evening a Marine came by sick bay and brought me some soup and crackers. I thanked him and he said, "Don't thank me, the platoon sergeant gave me the soup in the mess hall and told me to bring it to you." Just before lights were turned out, still another Marine dropped by to check on me and ask if I needed anything. And, of course, the sergeant had sent him, too.

I had erroneously thought that my platoon sergeant didn't care, but he did, and his concern became evident when he sent people to check on me and bring food. When I returned to my unit the following day, he acted as though nothing had happened. He continued to push me to my limits, but I knew that this tough Vietnam veteran had another side, too.

My platoon sergeant never became my pal or best friend, but from that day forward I knew that he had my back. Even though he himself did not attend to me in sick bay, he was personally involved in my well-being.

To draw a parallel between my Marine Corps sergeant and God may seem ridiculous (although my platoon sergeant would probably approve of the comparison), and I certainly don't want to push this analogy too far. Whatever motivations my sergeant had in showing me a bit of kindness cannot possibly be compared to God's love. God's love is unconditional and never fails, even when I do. In contrast, I think my platoon sergeant would have thrown me under a moving tank in a heartbeat if I had failed to live up to the ideals and standards of the Corps. His love was conditional, and every Marine knew it. Period. Yet, I have often wondered if the Marines who were instructed by my platoon sergeant to attend to me do not in some way represent how divine presence indirectly, even imperceptibly, slips into our lives.

If God can be revealed through "means of grace" such as the community of faith, the Bible and acts of love, then maybe God reveals divine presence through ordinary people like you and me, not because we are more deserving, but because we have come to know by God's grace that all individuals bear in their beings the image of God. Some people, unfortunately, have not yet become aware of that image. But for those who have embraced their responsibility as a "means of grace," God's presence can be experienced by others through their flawed and distorted images of that divine presence. Through earthly jars of clay God's presence may become real.

When I think of the possibility that divine presence might be experienced in other people's lives through human beings like me, I become acutely conscious that I am not here to live for myself. To think that I can be a gift of God's presence for others is an incredible honor and responsibility. Is it possible that God sends us to bring healing and comfort to those who have been abandoned or neglected, to those who have been damaged by life, to those who have lost hope or suffer without relief? Is God's personal nature most palpably experienced through the human touch? Can we find divine presence through human relationships?

RESPECTING GOD'S DISTANCE

Just as in biblical times, many people today have the feeling that God plays hide-and-seek with us. A pastor friend of mine, who I have known since high school, came to see me one afternoon with a heaviness of heart. We were not long into our conversation when he asked me if God was as remote in my life as God was in his. He felt as though God had deserted him, and now he was trying to care for people and steer them into a more meaningful life without any help from the very one who called him into ministry. A man who had spent more than thirty years leading churches, teaching people about God, caring for their needs and being present with them during good and bad times, felt in his own life that God had left him high and dry. I assured him I have often felt the same way. Haven't we all?

But do we have a right to expect anything more? If God was not readily accessible to Adam and Eve, the patriarchs or the psalmists, then we may assume our relationship with God will also know days when God appears rather distant, days when we live in the shadow of faith. Maybe we want something from God that is not in divine nature to give or not in our nature to receive. Maybe too much of God would be like looking directly into the sun, thus, God has to work around the edges to make divine presence known to us in more indirect and subtle ways. Of course, it is also possible that God intentionally distances divine presence from us the way a parent stands back when her child begins to take his first steps. For the child to transition from crawling to walking requires the parent to move away in order to allow the child to stand erect and walk on his own. There is, naturally, the risk the child might fall, but that is part of the growth process.

Then, too, the notion that we can know God directly in familiar, casual and intimate ways has marginal support in Scripture. Throughout the biblical story an encounter with God is usually associated with profound reverence, apprehension and distance. Israel did not even seek a direct experience with God, knowing the dangers of drawing too close to the divine nature (Exod. 20:19). By the time of Jesus an encounter with God often resulted in loss of sight or the inability to speak. To believe that we can approach God in a casual manner diminishes the mystery and awe that is representative of how we meet God in Scripture. In the biblical model God can be experienced, but usually not in direct ways and certainly not in the flippant or routine drive-by rendezvous embraced by so many in today's religious culture. An encounter with God necessitates a healthy dose of "fear and trembling" and is most often clouded by uncertainty, leaving ample room for both faith and doubt.

During my first pastorate a political leader in our town asked me to give an invocation at a political fundraiser. I was deeply skeptical that my prayer could rein in a rowdy group of political partisans, but I thought that it might at least offer a witness. Big mistake! While I prayed the overflow crowd barely paused from their raucous behavior. What was meant to be an act of worship became simply a filler on the program, a means to baptize the event with the illusion of religion before the main attraction. Casual familiarity may give the appearance of personal warmth, but too often what passes for casual is mere indifference. The idea of casual can imply that God is so ordinary that even an inattentive audience may experience divine presence.

When we read Scripture and hear of God's love, compassion, and concern, the intent is to help us grasp our value as human beings. God is not indifferent to the daily challenges and hardships we face. We creatures of flesh and blood matter to God. When the Bible declares that not a single bird falls from its nest unobserved by God, the message affirms that God is not uncaring toward us but is deeply immersed in our well-being. But acknowledging God's concern for us doesn't translate into flippant familiarity.

Maybe God's elusive nature is a means for us to come of age as human beings, to grow up, so to speak, to develop as responsible agents in order to fulfill our purpose as reflections of God's image in the world. I am not suggesting that we cannot experience God. It is true that a God who is divorced from everyday reality, who stands remotely apart from creation, would be of little consequence to us and certainly of no encouragement. On the contrary, I have come to believe that we can experience God's presence in warm and caring ways, just not in direct and unmediated ways.

So how can God's presence draw near to us? Is it even possible to enter into a meaningful experience with God? The answer may be right beside us.

EXPERIENCING GOD THROUGH HUMAN RELATIONSHIPS

The theologian Paul Tillich recognizes that human beings would not bother with any object of worship that was less than personal.[1] In language that can be abstract Tillich writes that since "God is the ground of everything personal. . . and carries within himself the ontological power of personality," the nature of God can be inferred through personal relationships.[2] In other words, Tillich believes God reveals divine presence by imbuing human beings with the capacity to engage in personal relationships with one another. Human beings, created in the image of God, an image that bears qualities of the personal, are divinely gifted to relate to each other in personal and intimate ways, and through authentic caring and compassionate social interaction can indirectly experience God's personal nature. The personal relationships we have with each other, relationships that we all too often take for granted, are in reality opportunities to enter into an experience with God. What a breathtaking concept! We can meet "face-to-face" with divine presence through common, ordinary, flesh-and-blood creatures, fellow human beings, who in some remarkable way bear God's image.

Generations of faith have recognized the mysterious nature of God's presence indirectly through human relationships, "for where two or three are gathered in my name, I am there among them" (Matt. 18:20 NRSV). In the scheme of creation we experience something of the personal nature of God through fellowship with one another. In both testaments God chooses to reveal divine presence primarily through community, and while not a direct, unmediated encounter, authentic human relationships have the power to open our eyes to divine presence.

Unfortunately, the potential for God to be present with us through meaningful relationships has been damaged by the sometimes willful disregard of the sacredness of life.[3] Martin Buber's classic *I and Thou* explains that the loss of God in the modern world is the consequence of our inability to engage in I-Thou relationships. Buber defines an I-Thou relationship as one where the relationship itself is the ultimate goal and not a means to an end. When we value other people as images of God and learn to discover something of God's presence within them, we are engaging in I-Thou relationships. We seek nothing from the other person but desire only to give ourselves in selfless acts of love. Obviously, there are risks in an I-Thou relationship. By an openness to reveal ourselves, we become vulnerable and may be hurt, but, if we are to experience God, the risk becomes the price we pay for the possibility of a divine encounter.

Most of our day-to-day relationships are shallow and superficial and have the air of brief and trivial encounters more than engaged relationships. Buber calls the relationships where the other person is treated as an object, a means to an end, an I-It relationship. An I-It relationship is detached and objective; an I-It relationship examines rather than experiences. Buber never disparages I-It relationships, for "without It man cannot live. . .but he who lives with It Alone is not a man" [person].[4] In I-It relationships the other person is never deeply valued, but only serves to help us accomplish a task or gratify our desires. There is little or no effort expended to experience the other person through heart-to-heart conversation, to exchange thoughts and feelings with another human being. To put it simply, an I-It relationship lacks meaningful and personal engagement.

Buber believes that our deep-seated loneliness is the result of these I-It encounters that dominate our human interactions, and because our lives are empty of meaningful connections, they are also empty of God's presence. God has been eclipsed, and in God's place we have settled for friends on Facebook or Twitter or other technological associations. But often these friendships are without depth and substance and only give the appearance of a relationship. We may have hundreds of people listed as friends on our Facebook account and still feel lonely. Like Adam, we are surrounded by all kinds of marvelous creatures, but because there is no one with whom we can share and commune with on a deep and personal level, we feel incomplete and alone.

Buber suggests an answer to our loneliness. When we learn to accept the other person as sacred and strive to value him/her in some mysterious way as an image of God, slowly, over time, a relationship may be forged that fills our emptiness and gives meaning to our lives. The Thou in Buber's book title represents not only the other person but also includes the world around us—nature, the animal kingdom and even the arts. Whenever we give ourselves, our entire being, to meeting the other as a subject and not merely an object, an I-Thou relationship becomes possible, whereby we can encounter the handiwork of God throughout the world. And in these encounters there is the hope of meeting God, for, as Buber notes, "in every Thou we address the eternal Thou."[5]

The importance of I-Thou relationships can hardly be overstated. For only in learning to engage in meaningful ways with other people can we learn what it means to be a human being ourselves, created in the image of God. The personalist John MacMurray writes:

The unit of personal existence is not the individual,
but two persons in personal relation; and that we are persons
not by individual right, but in virtue of our relation to one another.
The personal is constituted by personal relatedness.
The unit of the personal is not the "I," but the
"You and I." [6]

Only in community of two or more do we exist completely as human beings. An isolated individual is an incomplete self, for only in community of two or more do we fully reflect the image of our Creator. Apart from other people how can we possibly expect to experience a relationship with God?

Maybe the belief that we can enjoy a personal and direct relationship with God serves as a convenient substitute for having to make time to develop a personal relationship with our neighbor who lives across the street or a stranger who chooses to worship differently. An idealistic love for God can serve as a powerful distraction, permitting us to ignore the needs of those around us. Buber understands the selfish human nature well when he writes that many of us "would rather attend to God than to the world."[7] Attending to God requires little in the way of tangible acts of love but attending to our neighbor, especially the neighbor from a different faith perspective or cultural background, requires ongoing energy that often interrupts our cherished lifestyles of self-indulgence. A church leader once confided in me that he prayed for his neighbor, but he was reluctant to actually knock on his door and visit him. "He might think I want to be friends, he may want me to hang out with him or even invite my family over for dinner." It was far more convenient to "pray" for his neighbor than to risk an I-Thou relationship.

An I-Thou relationship with another human being comes with a steep price. A time commitment is involved, not to mention the emotional toll it takes to authentically engage with another human being. I-Thou relationships, while not predictable, don't just accidentally happen; they are intentionally cultivated. Our willingness to trust and be transparent to another person requires repeated life situations where confidence is gradually gained. We will endure hurt feelings, misunderstandings, and betrayals, and we will have to learn to forgive, compromise, and swallow our pride on occasion. I-Thou relationships are not without potential hazards. We proceed carefully, prayerfully, slowly and sometimes have to take a step back. In these relationships we seek no advantage over another person, no desire to put ourselves over someone else but strive only to love selflessly through empathy, compassion and patience.

An I-Thou relationship is demanding. We may feel that we don't have the time or stamina. Consequently, Buber stresses that I-Thou relationships eventually drift into I-It relationships. We are, after all, human beings and cannot live continually in the exacting relationship of the Thou. Our everyday social bonds with those closest to us simply cannot maintain the emotional toll of an I-Thou relationship. We are frail creatures, and we have physical and emotional limits. Therefore, I-It relationships play an important role in our lives because they make allowances for our humanity, but for us to encounter God our lives must consist of more than detached engagements. To put it bluntly, our human weaknesses must not be used as an excuse to bypass what is hard but necessary.

Because, according to Buber, all real living is meeting [I-Thou relationships], it is important to learn how to become fully present to our world.[8] We have spouses and children, jobs and schools, hobbies and private times. How can we possibly find the time to cultivate these deeper and more genuine relationships? It is a difficult challenge but one that is worth the effort. By the giving of ourselves to others and to the world in selfless acts of love, we open the door to a divine encounter.

So, how do we take the first steps? Maybe a few suggestions would help you get started. Remember that I-Thou relationships require intentionality as we do not superficially enter into them. Sometimes they unfold over a lifetime but, if we are attentive, having coffee with a new friend or engaging in meaningful conversation with a neighbor may evolve into an I-Thou relationship. Moreover, I-Thou relationships ebb and flow; we cannot control them or predict them. The important thing is to strive to be completely present to others. A good place to begin is at home. Strive to build I-Thou relationships with your spouse and your children or your mom and dad. If we do not seek to engage in close relationships with those nearest to us, then relationships with those outside the family may be a means to avoid the very elements inherent in an I-Thou relationship—vulnerability, selflessness, transparency, and intimacy. Family has a way of seeing us as we really are, and by learning to treat family members as sacred, we condition ourselves to be honest and open with others.

Make an effort to see the best in people. My years in ministry taught me that every person has good qualities and areas where work needs to be done. We are all projects under construction. Sometimes we meet people who make poor first impressions, but if we don't give up on these people, we may discover a lonely and interesting human being in need of our love and kindness. Time and again in my work as pastor I have seen the warmth of human kindness melt the most hardened heart.

Be open to surprise friendships. Years ago I became acquainted with a man who mowed lawns for a living. He worked hard and struggled every day to make ends meet. He was of a different race and his background looked nothing like mine. I have had a wealth of opportunities; he has had few. Over time we became friends, and the friendship on occasion rose to an I-Thou relationship. He was a lay minister, and my wife and I would regularly visit his church to hear him preach. We often had lunch together where we shared from deep within our hearts. We laughed about our cultural differences, prayed about similar struggles, and discussed theological issues.

He died not long ago from cancer while only in his mid-fifties. I will carry his memory with me for as long as I live. His friendship was a serendipitous surprise, and my life experienced a touch of God through this unexpected relationship.

There are countless ways to engage with people and build I-Thou relationships, but the most important thing is to be alert, attentive, and sensitive to the people around us and continually remind ourselves that we often entertain angels unaware. God's presence may visit us through the life of a stranger or maybe an adversary or even the person we have known all our lives.

When we are willing to meet the demands for an I-Thou relationship, we invite the possibility of God into our lives. We may not even be aware that divine presence visited us during these moments, and only afterwards in hindsight are we sometimes able to look back and recognize that God was there. These experiences may not have provided a direct unmediated encounter with God, but by exercising faith, we may have sensed a transcending presence.

An afternoon or evening with my wife or our two grown sons can turn into a sacred moment, a moment filled with Holy presence. These times are seldom anticipated. They just happen. Usually, only in retrospect am I able to reflect that the occasion, while routine and rather ordinary, also exceeded the normal pattern of life. In each case, at first the time was simply special to me, but as I continued to dwell on the experience special became sacred. Over the years I have developed friendships with people, both young and old, with whom I could sense divine presence. We may have gathered around a table to share a meal or we may have gazed at the stars on a cloudless night or talked of trivial matters when suddenly we became sensitive to the sacredness of the moment. Or maybe weeks after the experience the memory continued to bless me, and I realized only then that the moment was filled with divine presence.

These remembrances are embedded deeply within me and when my faith journey staggers in unrelenting darkness, they serve to awaken my sluggish consciousness that even in the shadow we can know something of God's goodness. Even when it seems as though nothing but emptiness and despair fill each day, I-Thou relationships connect us to Sacred Presence, for wherever two or three are gathered together there exists the possibility of God and with the possibility of God, there is hope.

I am painfully aware that one of my greatest failings is that my circle of friends tends to be too narrow, too insular. I have grown comfortable with certain people and to stretch myself, I need to be open to new meaningful relationships. I continually remind myself to be alert to the people who cross my path. For I know if I cut myself off from others—those who rub me the wrong way or vote differently than I do—I risk cutting myself off from God. By continuing to enlarge my boundaries, my relationship with God is strengthened and I become a more complete person. Seldom am I consciously aware that through these relationships my own spiritual growth is taking place.

Whatever term we choose to use in reference to our experience with God, I am convinced that without empathetic and selfless engagement with other people life with God will be less than personal. God's most consistent entrance into our lives happens in community of two or more. While the life of faith includes times of isolation and loneliness, these periods are only temporary. A long-term absence from fellow human beings ensures that we soon lose touch with God—for in every Thou we encounter the eternal Thou.

CHAPTER 9

THE GOD BEYOND GOD

We are in greater need of a proof for the
authenticity of faith than of the proof for the
existence of God.

- Abraham Heschel

One Saturday afternoon I spent several hours in a bookstore browsing through the religious section. Long rows of packed shelves displayed religious themes on almost every conceivable subject. I picked up a book with an interesting title, glanced at the table of contents, and then thumbed through the pages, pausing here and there to read a paragraph or two. I put the book back on the shelf and grabbed another and repeated the process. I was fascinated by the wide variety of religious topics and perspectives and quickly lost track of time. There were books on how to raise children in a godly home and books on how to develop a Christian marriage. There were books on biblical history and theology. There were books on Hinduism and Islam, books on Judaism and Hasidic traditions—a smorgasbord of theological delight. I would have remained in the store until closing, but my wife came for me to remind me that we had a dinner engagement and needed to leave.

Books that treat religious and spiritual themes continue to be highly popular in today's culture. Even though confidence in religious institutions has declined all across the country in recent years, we continue to hunger for spiritual experiences, something that connects us to that which is beyond us, a higher power or a supernatural revelation that gives meaning to life. Interest in the spiritual realm in our highly technological and advanced culture has soared.

The continuing thirst for the spiritual life does not surprise me. It is part of our nature to seek that which is greater than ourselves. Augustine recognized our longing for God when he wrote in his *Confessions* that we cannot rest until we have surrendered to God. Unfortunately, this desire or yearning for that which is greater than ourselves also has a potential downside—we too easily succumb to false gods who promise instant and continuous spiritual enlightenment or gratification. Like the person desperately desiring to lose weight tries every new dietary fad on the market, people seeking God often become impatient with God's elusive nature and fall victim to the latest promise of spiritual fulfillment.

There are no quick fixes in life with God. For us to know divine presence more is required than thumbing through a few pages of some religious book. The prophet Jeremiah reminds us that God can only be found when you seek the Holy with all your heart (Jer. 29:13). I understand Jeremiah to be saying that God's presence can become a reality in our lives, but only if we are willing to make God the center of our lives.

But how do we do that? If God becomes the focus of all that we are, don't we risk becoming so heavenly minded that we are of no earthly good? Not necessarily. There is a consistent thread running throughout Scripture that the primary way to meet God is through human relationships, more specifically through I-Thou relationships. Actually by reaching out to others in selfless acts of love, we not only move forward to make God the focal point of our lives, but we also build a better world. The biblical emphasis on caring and compassionate human relationships, as a means to draw us closer to God, should not be underestimated.[1]

The core biblical belief of both Judaism and Christianity maintains that no one can directly experience God.[2] The biblical injunction that no person can see God's face and live implies that God makes divine presence known to us only indirectly (Exod. 33:20). In other words, we come to an awareness of God through analogy and symbolism; relational terms like Father, Lord, and

Savior help us to develop an image and understanding of God that allow us to connect to what our minds could not otherwise perceive. Without I-Thou relationships we would lack these analogies that make possible an understanding of what God is like. Thus I-Thou relationships are means of grace that allow us to encounter divine presence.

While I-Thou relationships entail valuing the other person as a subject and not an object, these relationships are not limited to special occasions or even special people, but include the meeting of others in the normal routines of life. These relationships are not necessarily mystical or even supernatural; they are meetings where we fully engage with the other person by completely opening ourselves to their presence. I find that kind of engagement extremely challenging but also deeply life affirming.

It is far more convenient to read my Bible or pray in solitude than to engage with my neighbor on a meaningful level. If I believe that I can have direct access to God apart from community, then my neighbor loses significance, but if I yearn for God and know that through I-Thou relationships divine presence can be experienced, then my sense of social responsibility takes on infinitely greater importance. Is it possible that our fractured society, that we frequently blame on divisive politics and disparate social values, actually derives from our failure to engage in I-Thou relationships? When we are at odds with anyone who doesn't look like us or think like us or believe like us, how can we possibly encounter God? Maybe our predilection for gods who make no demands on us and are easily accessible and knowable has become a substitute for the more demanding life with the biblical God who challenges us to engage in I-Thou relationships with our fellow human beings.

GOD IS, WELL, GOD

If we believe that we can have a direct and unmediated relationship with God, belief can easily devolve into casual familiarity or even idolatry.[3] The Bible teaches that God is always the wholly Other. We never get to know God the way we do a friend or a spouse. It is true that there may be times when we sense a closeness or intimacy with God and these feelings can comfort us. We may feel God's presence in our lives and whisper prayers to God throughout the day. In these sacred moments we may call God "Father." But there are also times when we may feel that God is distant and inaccessible, and during these occasions it is as though our prayers do not rise above the ceiling. We may feel alone or even abandoned. We soon learn that experiences with God are not predictable. The writer Christian Wiman insightfully adds, "The moment you begin to speak with certitude about God, he is gone."[4]

When we think about it, we realize that we know practically nothing about God. We may glean some insights into God by reading the Bible and other holy writings, and we may deduce certain limited aspects of God from creation. Even the Bible, however, presents a view of God that underscores how radically different God is from human beings. The biblical prophet Isaiah writes that God's thoughts are not our thoughts and God's ways are not our ways (Isa. 55:8-9). The Bible makes clear that we cannot know God the way we can know each other. Paul echoes this sentiment when he writes that when it comes to understanding the ways of God we look through a dark glass, unable to see clearly (1 Cor. 13:12). In life with God we walk by faith, not by sight. Consequently, one of faith's closest companions is humility.

During my ministry serving churches I grew concerned about people who pushed their claim of a personal relationship with God too far. When we believe that our experience with God gives us spiritual insight that no one else has, we have gone too far. When we believe that God excuses our immoral or unethical behavior because we have a special relationship with God, we have gone too far. When we believe that our interpretation of Scripture is the only correct one, we have gone too far. When we believe God is only on our side, we have gone too far.

Humility may be one of the most important characteristics of faith. To know that our understanding of God may be wrong opens the door to the possibility of greater spiritual growth. Only when we approach God as beggars, with receptive hearts, can we be spiritually nourished. Pride and arrogance may give us a temporary feeling of power and accomplishment, but ultimately we are left spiritually malnourished.

Thomas Aquinas, who lived in the thirteenth-century, is considered one of the most brilliant theologians of the church. His writings are still read and valued by both Catholics and Protestants. One day, after a lifetime of prayer, study, meditation and writing, he threw down his pen and announced, "All that I have written seems like straw." He never wrote again. Exactly what was in Aquinas' mind when he wrote these words merits debate, but I think that this giant of a theologian came to realize that compared to the reality of God, human understanding has barely scratched the surface.

WORSHIP WITHOUT HUMILITY IS DANGEROUS

Exodus 32 serves as a good example of how a narrow perspective of what it means to have a personal relationship with God can actually drive us further away from God. An insatiable desire for a god who is easily accessible and knowable can cause significant damage in the life of faith by creating a pleasant but dangerous illusion of God's presence.

The chapter opens with Israel encamped at the foot of Mount Sinai. Their leader, Moses, has climbed the mountain to meet with God. After a while, the people grew impatient waiting for their absent leader. There were many challenges to their survival, food and water not the least of them. Day after day passed and still Moses did not come down. The people began to grumble. They lived in a wilderness of uncertainty and the God of Moses seemed far away, while their material and spiritual needs were close at hand. In a time of desperation people will reach for anything that promises hope, even if that hope is chimerical.

The people solicited Aaron, the brother of Moses, to fashion for them an object upon which they could focus, an object to distract them from their feelings of abandonment. They gave Aaron their possessions of gold, which Aaron melted down and formed into a calf.

They convinced themselves that what they had done was pleasing to God, and the next day they celebrated "a festival to the Lord" (Exod. 32:5 NRSV). The Israelites disobeyed God by creating an idol, and now justified their actions by claiming that the golden calf was an aid to worship! When our god becomes an object of familiarity, license for the most bizarre religious behavior becomes acceptable. A self-created god offers no resistance to self-indulgence, only confirmation. A god who is conveniently accessible easily morphs into a golden calf.

There is a trace of humor in the story as well. When Moses returned and saw what Israel had done he was furious. He demanded an explanation from his brother, Aaron, and his sheepish brother replied that the people insisted on the idolatrous act. As for his part, Aaron, with a straight face no doubt, claims he had little to do with it. The people gave me their gold, I simply threw it into the fire and miraculously "out came the calf" (Exod. 32:24 NRSV).

The story illustrates our greedy craving for a god who is familiar and close at hand, and, of course, an idol is always present and always personal;

one can see and feel a false god. An idol is always there when we need it. An idol does our bidding and holds to the same convictions and beliefs that we do, votes the same way and sees the world through our perspective. Gods who are fashioned by our imagination and prejudices are gods we are comfortable with—they demand little from us, promise everything but deliver virtually nothing.

False gods are serious rivals to authentic faith. Created gods never challenge the status quo; they are the status quo. They are widely popular for they mirror our desires and arrogance. Idols provide a degree of religious stability, for they are always predictable. There is little mystery to the gods we manufacture for they are mere reflections of the self, created in our own image.

Israel struggled, just as we do, with creating and worshipping false gods who gave the illusion of divine presence. Even the disciples, not able to comprehend the ways of Jesus, tried to interpret him in ways that fit their religious ideology. They believed that Jesus would usher in an age of prosperity and renewed national power. They were convinced that Jesus would inaugurate God's kingdom on earth, but by rigidly trying to place Jesus in a box, refusing to acknowledge his unpredictable divine nature, they succeeded only in creating greater distance between themselves and God.

Pushing a personal relationship with God to the extreme all too easily slips into self-worship, and self-worship is undoubtedly the greatest threat to authentic faith. We may blissfully bow before the altar, thinking all the while that we are kneeling before the Almighty, but in fact we may be paying homage to the self. Of course we would never consciously worship an idol, but whenever we become too comfortable with God, too secure in our relationship, we risk creating a false god.

EXERCISING HUMILITY IN FAITH

The Christian mystic Meister Eckhart was keenly aware that false gods or illusions of divine presence pose legitimate threats to authentic faith. According to Eckhart, if we are to live life with God we must continually strive for "the God beyond God."[5] I understand Eckhart to be saying that every day we must evaluate our faith anew, for even the community of faith can be wrong as evidenced by both Israel and the church over and over again. Yesterday's faith experience may have been only a self-reflection. Today, we must open ourselves to fresh insights into how God may be present in our lives, and when we think we have entered into God's presence, maybe we should respond first by exercising humility and ask ourselves if we have settled on an object of worship which looks and thinks too much like we do.

If we are to live life with God and avoid worshipping phantom gods, there are two critical questions to keep in mind. First, is the object of my worship compelling me to be a better human being—more loving toward my neighbor, more unselfish, more compassionate toward those in need? False gods turn us inward, toward a self-centered and egotistical mindset. We habitually settle for false gods because idols make no demands on us, and we control them. If my neighbor is in need, then I can pass the buck without the slightest hesitation because my created god requires nothing of me. Let someone else lend a hand, we tell ourselves, he is not my responsibility. A god of my own creation does not compel me to make sacrifices for others.

The God of Abraham, the God of Moses, and the God of Jesus, on the other hand, calls us to commit to the demands of faith. We are to do what is right and good in our relationships with other people, according to Mosaic Law (Deut. 6:18). In the New Testament Jesus taught that authentic faith has practical effects—acts of love—giving a cup of water to someone who is thirsty, bread to the hungry, and other acts of compassion. To emphasize the broad range of acts of love Jesus tells the story of the Good Samaritan to illustrate that our relationship with God is borne out by the tangible expressions of concern we practice toward others.

An expert of the law comes to Jesus and questions him what he must do to inherit eternal life. Jesus replies that he must love God and love his neighbor. The lawyer further queries Jesus by asking, "And who is my neighbor?" The lawyer may have reasoned, as was common in the Judaism of the day, that neighbor included only the person of like faith, a fellow Jew. In response Jesus tells the story of the Good Samaritan, a story that demonstrates that "neighbor" is defined as encompassing all human beings, even those who have different religious beliefs. Jesus concludes that the one who shows practical acts of love toward neighbor will receive life with God. In this New Testament teaching our relationship with God depends on our relationship with other human beings, including those who are not of our faith, through thoughtful expressions of compassion. For Jesus the ultimate question is not "Who is my neighbor?" but rather "Am I a good neighbor?" The demands of faith call us to live selflessly and humbly toward all others in imitation of the Jesus way.

The teachings of Jesus, emphasizing the importance of human relationships, echo the crucial themes of the Old Testament and rabbinic tradition. Later, when Jesus was asked by one of his own followers the way to God he replied, "I am the way and the truth and the life. No one comes to the Father except through me" (John 14:6 NRSV). This verse has often been interpreted in an exclusionary manner that only those who believe in Jesus will enter into life with God. To believe, therefore, means to accept the historical reality of Jesus, the resurrection and that Jesus is God's Messiah. By intellectually subscribing to these beliefs, we enter into everlasting life with God. I do not think that this rendering captures what Jesus is teaching his disciples.

In context, Jesus invites people to a particular way of life, the Jesus way. "Follow me," he calls out to those curious about his way of life. The life of faith, according to Jesus, is not only about believing but about a certain way of living. Just believing would have been meaningless to first century people. The word "believe" in the world of Jesus was not merely an intellectual term but was associated with commitment and action. When Jesus challenges us to "believe" in him, he is summoning us to imitate his way of life, his way of treating people, and his sacrificial way of living.

By following in his footsteps, so to speak, we will discover the true meaning of life. If we desire to experience the presence of God, then we begin by following the way of Jesus—a way marked by compassion, love, and forgiveness toward others. By following the way we will discover the truth. The truth is that loving concern for other human beings enriches our life as well as the lives of those around us. Then by following the way of Jesus and discovering the truth we will be drawn to that for which our hearts yearn—life that transcends mundane existence. In other words, when Jesus invites us to follow him he is not providing a formula to gain heaven; he is revealing a path for life with God. Jesus seeks primarily, in my understanding, not to get us into heaven, but to get heaven into us. The more we selflessly engage with other human beings through acts of sacrificial love, the greater the possibility of life with God.

There is a second critical question to ask ourselves as we strive for the God beyond God in order to defend against the worship of a false god: does my object of worship move me to accept my human limitations? Authentic faith never loses a self-critical perspective. We must continually remind ourselves that our faith convictions may be wrong. Intellectual and spiritual humility characterize genuine worship.

Many people, unfortunately, are more comfortable with a counterfeit god than the God who continually challenges them to rise above their petty prejudices and limited perspectives. A counterfeit god condones and encourages dogmatic faith assertions. False gods forbid critical reflection about what we believe as rationalism is considered the enemy of the supernatural. Miguel de Unamuno tells the story of a Parisian doctor who changed the location of his practice when he discovered a quack healer in the area was stealing his patients. In his new location, where his credentials as a physician were unknown, he pawned himself off as a magic healer. Soon people were flocking to his office thinking that his cures were supernatural.

When it was finally learned that he was not a quack, but a real doctor, he acknowledged that he had hid the truth from his patients because they preferred a fake who healed through the supernatural rather than an authentic physician. [6]

It is human nature to gravitate toward the path of least resistance to escape our anxieties and fears. Often it is not truth we seek but release from a troubled and fear-filled life. Whatever provides the greatest source of comfort at the lowest cost or effort readily works its way into our lives as an object of devotion. But rationalism is not the enemy of faith. The Quaker philosopher Elton Trueblood reminds us that faith without reason is mere superstition. Prayerfully examining our faith claims in community throughout our lives does not drive us away from God but helps us to distinguish true spiritual paths from false ones.

IF NOT HIGHER

The writer Isaac Lieb Peretz tells a wonderful rabbinic story of a beloved rabbi who on the Day of Atonement would disappear for a number of hours. One of his devoted followers believed that the rabbi was secretly meeting with God so when the rabbi left the synagogue, his devoted student followed closely behind him. He watched as the rabbi removed his fine rabbinic clothes and attired himself with coarse peasant garments. The rabbi then walked to a lowly cottage where a disabled woman lived and entered her house.

The curious follower watched the rabbi through the window as he cared for the old and sick woman. The rabbi cleaned the room, prepared a meal, and visited with the invalid. When the rabbi's disciple returned to the synagogue, he was asked by the members where the rabbi had gone. "Did the rabbi ascend to heaven?" the people asked. He looked at the inquiring congregation and then said, "If not higher." [7]

We ascend to God through human relationships and acts of kindness or maybe I should say, God descends to us. The beloved disciple penned the words, "No one has ever seen God; but if we love each other, God lives in us and his love is made complete in us" (1 John 4:12). Still, just because we quote some passage in the Bible does not necessarily validate our belief. Only when the biblical words help us to build a better world, a world where violence and hatred give way to peace and understanding, will we know then that there is power in those words. God may be elusive and God's ways mysterious, but whenever love is put into practice, there is hope and hope offers the possibility of life with God.

We cannot see God, but we can see each other, and it is the person we see who challenges the authenticity of our faith. For it is much easier to love a substitute god than it is to love the neighbor who allows his trash to blow into our yard.

CHAPTER 10

WHEN FEELINGS AREN'T ENOUGH

A story does not ask for a decision.
Instead, it asks for identification,
which is how transformation begins

- Barbara Brown Taylor

Have you ever had an experience where you sensed that God was with you or maybe you felt God was behind the scenes orchestrating some specific event in your life to a favorable outcome? A friend of mine calls these serendipitous interruptions "God moments." At one time or another many of us have experienced these comforting surprises. When God moments occur we may perceive them to be personal, even intimate. These times may be incredibly uplifting as they often transcend the humdrum of everyday existence. We may sense a God moment when we see our newborn baby for the first time or when we receive news that the test results came back negative or when our boss gives us a badly needed raise. A God moment may occur when we have dinner with friends or when we listen to rapturous music on a quiet moonlit evening. Even a hike in a tree-studded forest may trigger feelings of God's nearness as we gaze in wonder at the majesty of creation.

We seldom anticipate God moments. We can't really prepare for them. They drift into our lives unannounced, like the soft brush of a gentle breeze across our face, and when our hearts are opened to these gifts, we are filled with indescribable gratitude. Like children on Christmas morning, we feel only the joy of the present.

Feelings go hand-in-hand with being human. Religion is often criticized as mere emotion devoid of rational analysis, but any human experience, any area of life that is meaningful to us, has an emotional side. Take away the passion and human beings are left not with clear-eyed objective truth, but with indecipherable data disconnected from the world of flesh and blood. While a dispassionate approach to religious belief may sound more intellectually honest, the interpretative process, infused by feelings and emotions, plays a significant role in every area of human importance, including religion. Religious belief empty of passion betrays not the intellect but what it means to be human.

God moments lean heavily on the lyrical side, and rightly so, for there is nothing more deserving of our passions and feelings than possible life with God. We would have to be machines to restrain our emotions with so much at stake.

When we experience a surprising act of grace, a God moment, we can feel as though we have in some mysterious way been touched by God. We probably cannot explain these moments of grace; they are mysterious interventions that break into the routine patterns of life, and, if we examine them too closely, we may convince ourselves that they are nothing more than common and ordinary happenings. How utterly human to overlook God's disguised presence in the everyday stuff of life, like a burning bush or a baby born in a manger. Maybe a better approach would be to thankfully embrace God moments as gifts and allow them to warm our hearts. When trapped in a melancholy shadow, light may suddenly appear, easing our anxieties and fears of the darkness. These welcomed incursions are not permanent, but they can add spiritual fuel to a life running on fumes.

A few months after my ongoing cancer treatments my oncologist called to tell me that my tumor markers were elevated, a potentially ominous signal that the malignancy was metastasizing throughout my body. That night while my family slept I wandered around our house thinking that my life might soon end. How would my wife make it without my financial support? Who would play catch with our boys or commiserate with them when their first teenage love was unrequited? Who would be there for them when they needed a dad? My heart was pounding with adrenaline. After my earlier surgeries, I had thought the worst was behind me; now once again I was faced with the prospect of premature death. I tried to sit still in a chair in our den and pray that God would give me the courage to gracefully accept whatever the future held, but I was restless. Throughout the night I paced back and forth in our small family room. At times I prayed but mostly I just stared into what seemed like an empty void, a dark universe of hopelessness.

At some point I began to make out picture frames on the den walls, and I realized that dawn was beginning to break. I could see the first signs of morning glimmering under the curtains. I heard the grandfather clock chime in the background. Then, slowly, I became aware that my anxiety had eased. I no longer felt my heart pounding within my chest, a sense of calm had settled over me. I tried to think at what hour during the night my troubled soul had found rest, but I could not recall the moment. I only knew that once I saw the morning light, I no longer feared the darkness. I sensed no assurance that I would be healed of my cancer, but from that moment, I was at peace. Whether I lived or died, I was content to leave my fate in God's hands.

In the few times I have shared this experience with other people, it always sounds rather unspectacular, even mundane. Nothing really happened, at least nothing that I can pinpoint. I saw no visions, nor did I witness anything remotely unusual. I heard no voices or sounds from on high. I experienced no grand epiphany or promise of healing. From a purely objective perspective nothing out of the ordinary took place. Still, in spite of the absence of spectacular fireworks, the memory serves as a wonderful God moment for me.

Sometimes when the shadow grows darker I question my God moment. I think of all kinds of factors that might have soothed my restless spirit that night. Maybe my morning transformation was due to fatigue from not having slept. Maybe psychologically I had prepared myself for death. I am not discounting these possible explanations, but way down deep I believe divine presence visited me and in some unknown way released me from the power of fear.

More than thirty years have passed since that wondrous event took place, yet whenever my faith begins to falter for whatever reason, the memory of that experience has a way of bubbling to the surface, providing a sense of relief that soothes and calms my troubled heart. With each passing day, however, that remembrance becomes more translucent, and I fear that one day the memory will fade like an early morning dream, and it will no longer have the mystical power it once did. In short, my God moment can't furnish the kind of day-to-day support I need for the challenging life of faith, and as meaningful as the experience was, that moment of grace is too slippery, too intangible, to provide lasting strength for my ongoing journey.

Life is difficult and unfair, and, if the only pillar of faith we have to stand on is the memory of an ineffable mystery, it is only a matter of time before that pillar collapses. Our remembered private moments with God may seem thin and barely discernible during the cold and barren seasons of faith. There will be times, especially in the face of life's unexplainable horrors, when God moments are simply not enough and when our God moments slip away, we may feel as though God has turned away from us.

God moments are like wedding anniversaries—beautiful occasions for celebration, but by themselves not enough to build a marriage. Success-ful marriages require more than an annual highpoint; solid relationships depend on what we do the other 364 days of the year. A wonderful anniver-sary dinner is an event to savor, but without both partners working to build a marital bond throughout the year, that grand memory slowly dims, leaving only shadowy remnants of what once was.

Similar to a marriage there are no short-cuts to life with God. God mo-ments can be spiritually energizing for a faith commitment that has grown weary with the day-to-day challenges of life. After all, in the marathon of faith there are protracted times when the unrelenting ordinariness of life may numb us to any sense of divine presence, and during those long arid stretches God moments can refresh our parched spirits and put a bounce back in our step.

We have all had experiences when we sensed a transcending presence or at least wondered in awe at some unexplained mystery. Some people may just chalk these moments up to the fluctuating emotions of human nature, but a person of faith may interpret these breaks with the routine as di-vine encounters. Throughout my ministry people have often related to me some moment or event that became a source of assurance or hope during a stressful time. They believed God drew near them, that they experienced a God moment. These special sensations should not be ridiculed or devalued as mere emotional episodes. People on the receiving end of God moments are sincere that something significant and wonderful happened, and they interpret the event as an in-breaking of God into their lives. I can rejoice and celebrate with those who have felt a brush of grace, for when these moments ease into our lives, the shadow recedes, and we may see hopeful signs of light, at least for the moment. Still, the journey of faith eventually will stall and darkness will inevitably descend, and to find strength to push on we need something more than momentary feelings, regardless of how uplifting.

GOD MOMENTS VERSUS SACRED STORIES

As significant as God moments are, they cannot construct a strong enough foundation for an enduring faith. If we rely merely on God moments to shape our faith journey, our relationship with God will be limited by those experiences, and we will cut ourselves off from countless other channels that might strengthen faith and contribute additional insight into what it means to live life with God.

To sustain a faith journey we need something more to guide us as we seek life with God, a more enlightened course that doesn't depend solely on emotions and feelings. While emotions play an important role in the life of faith, they can easily mislead us when the going gets tough, especially when cold, dark winds have snuffed out any sense of God's warmth. Is there anything that will help us maintain our spiritual balance when the bottom falls out of our world, and even the memories of our cherished God moments can no longer comfort us?

I was twenty-eight-years-old, fresh out of seminary, and pastoring my first church when early one Monday morning, a few days before Christmas, a member of the church called and asked me to check on her elderly friend, Annie Mae. I quickly dressed and drove to the home of Annie Mae. I rang the doorbell several times but no one answered. I tried to open the door and was surprised to discover the door was unlocked. I cracked the door a few inches and called Annie Mae's name. No response.

I could see a purse lying on the dining room table and thought she might be in the back yard. I walked around the house to the garage, which was unattached to the house, and I looked through the garage window to see if her car might be gone. When I saw the car, I opened the side door and walked in. I immediately saw a figure slumped over the steering wheel. I took a step or two closer and then froze. The glass was shattered on the driver's side where the bullet had exited after going through Annie Mae's head. The scene was gruesome. I had seen combat film in the Marine Corps and had some understanding of the ugliness of violence, but this was different. I was not in a combat zone; I was a pastor making a house call. I zoned out for several seconds, not able to fully comprehend the scene before me, then I ran into the house and called the police. An autopsy later revealed that she had been dead for at least a day, maybe longer.

I went home and told my wife what had happened. I had only been a pastor for a couple of months, and what I had just witnessed deeply distressed me. I could not sponge away the graphic image of Annie Mae's suicide, and whatever God moments I had stored within me were incapable of bringing relief. Why had I not seen signs of her depression? I could not even remember for certain the last time I saw her. My congregation was small, and I blamed myself for not being more attentive to a lonely and distraught old woman.

Throughout that Christmas season and for months afterwards, I continued to struggle with Annie Mae's death. There was an emptiness within me, as if all my spiritual marrow had been hollowed out. I doubted my fitness for ministry and at times felt like an accomplice to her death. I repeatedly replayed every conversation I could remember with her. Why had I been so blind, so deaf? I recognized I was depressed, but I thought that by throwing myself into my pastoral duties the darkness would eventually lift. It didn't.

A sense of spiritual resignation overwhelmed me. I just wanted to run away, to find a place where no one knew I was a pastor. I questioned my faith and convinced myself that if I were truly a believer, I would not be having these confusing thoughts, bouts with depression and constant doubts. Maybe there was something lacking within me? Maybe God had abandoned me?

Every day I spent time in Scripture, reading passages from both testaments searching for answers, some light that might show me the way out of my darkness. As I read from the Psalms I became aware of how often the phrases "Why have you turned your face away from me?" and "How long, O Lord? Will you forget me forever?" appear in these ancient prayers. I had read these verses many times before, but now they took on a heightened relevance. Slowly, I began to realize that feelings of melancholy and despair abound in the Bible. People in the Bible struggled with feelings of emptiness and spiritual abandonment much to the same degree that I was experiencing. I read their prayers of heartbreak as if they were my own. Identifying with these ancient people of faith, I no longer felt so alone, so bereft of soulmates. And ever so slowly I began to emerge from my cave of darkness, not completely into the light, but at least sense that I was moving toward it or maybe it was moving toward me.

All too often the church presents a rosy picture of faith. Within the church culture it is often said that if we just have faith in God, God will shield us from evil. Reading the biblical stories, however, helped me to discover that the life of faith has never been all sunshine and fair weather. There has never been a time when those who ventured life with God experienced only azure skies and perpetual good fortune. The heroic figures of Scripture knew well the gray, overcast days of faith when all appeared lost and God far away.

As I studied the stories of other men and women who also labored in the shadow, I found myself being drawn into their world, participating in their faith journey. Their soulful pleas and confessions became more than historical accounts about people who questioned their God experience; their stories validated my own spiritual crisis by helping me to see that my faith was not weak—it was real. To know that biblical men and women experienced dark days where God seemed far away encouraged me that what I was going through was not all that unusual. When I read where the psalmists pleaded for God to return, it was as though they were speaking for me, voicing my thoughts and prayers. When Job criticized God for being unfair, callous and even deceitful, I found a soulmate who had walked in my shoes. When Jeremiah felt that God had abandoned him, I nodded my head in understanding. It was as though we were close friends, whispering in hushed tones about our disappointment with God. I commiserated with John the Baptist who felt confused and maybe even misled when his expectations of Messiah didn't materialize. I knew the feeling.

These stories spoke to me and gave me hope because they were so wonderfully human. These biblical figures had weak links in their faith just as I do. They were not superheroes immune to skepticism and doubt, and, because they were real people, their faith experiences resonated with me and became Sacred Stories that filled my emptiness with hope. The Sacred Stories reached me on a deeper and more enduring level than what God moments I had experienced. These stories had withstood the most severe trials and continue to serve as authentic spiritual guides for people like me, who have lost their way. They encouraged me not to be ashamed of my weakness and my humanity; they gave me permission to question not only my faith but also God without fear of divine reprisals. While the stories enlightened me to expect dark and lonely times in life with God, they also gave me strength to never give in to hopelessness. I was the novice and they were the seasoned travelers, who candidly shared the highs and lows of their faith adventures. Their spiritual journeys revealed tried and true paths that offer sage counsel in how to survive feelings of God's withdrawal from our lives. I realized that the more melancholic Sacred Stories were not written to discourage but were preserved and valued because they were real accounts of how faith journeys may unexpectedly slide from cheerful optimism to gloomy depression. It became clear to me that by acknowledging the shadow side of life with God, I would be better prepared for the inevitable roller coaster of faith.

I further learned that Sacred Stories encompass far more than just bleak tales of dark days and cold nights. Sacred Stories reveal all variations of faith. More hopeful Sacred Stories remind us that even though our life may be in the throes of despair, and we may have lost all hope and given up on God, we are not alone. We are part of a community, a community that has walked in our shoes, thought our thoughts and sympathizes with what we are going through. That faith community stands shoulder to shoulder with us, and by doing so, moderates the harshest effects of feeling abandoned by God. For countless generations these Sacred Stories have pulled people back from the brink of hopelessness. They have encouraged those in the dark places of life that they do not suffer alone and warned those glibly embracing blessing after blessing that the fragility of faith is all too real.

The Sacred Stories have a way of speaking to us regardless of where we are in our faith journey. Figures like Abraham, Moses, Jeremiah, Isaiah, the psalmists, Jesus, Paul, and many others reveal that real faith knows both euphoric highs and discouraging lows. These narratives open our eyes to a larger faith picture by providing a far more meaningful foundation than the reassuring but often transitory God moments.

Many of the Sacred Stories may have begun as God moments but over the course of time these valued experiences garnered credibility by being recognized by the community of faith as spiritual happenings far more significant than private touches of grace. The Sacred Stories added a significant layer of theological support that formed a more reliable basis for faith. Needing a more secure foundation, people over the centuries saw the power within these stories that could nourish faith journeys throughout all the turbulent seas of life. The stories were remembered, passed down orally and later written down, and, along with other writings, became what we know today as the Bible.

God moments, while still valued, especially by the recipients, became secondary to the Sacred Stories. People hungering for spiritual direction found in the Sacred Stories trustworthy guides for life with God. These historical narratives not only reveal how previous generations of faith survived the lonely and bitter adventures of faith, but they also rejoice with those celebrating divine presence. These stories rose above the feelings and emotions of God moments by giving a more substantial and sustainable account of how entire communities experienced God. Let me briefly explain the differences between God moments and Sacred Stories.

HOW SACRED STORIES DIFFER FROM GOD MOMENTS

First, God moments are individual experiences that are rooted in emotions. They may be shared with other people and may even be a source of
unabashed joy, but the private nature of the God moment makes the experience exclusive. A God moment is "my" story, not "our" story. Other people
are on the outside looking in, like spectators at a football game. Spectators
do not actually participate, though they may cheer, their primary place is in
the stands, not on the playing field.

Sacred Stories, on the other hand, are inclusive narratives that are
intended for everyone. There is little private about them. They are meant to
give reference points for the faith adventure by helping us to identify with
our spiritual heritage. In Sacred Stories we can read ourselves into the story.
We don't just watch from the stands; we are wooed to participate in the con-
test, to actively engage. Sacred Stories represent "our" story, a story broad
enough to include all of us—where no nation, race or people are excluded.

Second, God moments usually have little moral or ethical direction. Their
purpose is to encourage, not instruct. We all have human weaknesses and regardless of who we are, we need boundaries and moral and ethical guidelines.
God moments may offer warm and cozy feelings, but what they don't provide
is wise counsel for the life of faith. God moments are inherently unstable
because they depend solely on human emotions. We are feeling-oriented
beings that are guided by our individual self-interests. God moments tend to
promote our self-interests and, in the process, create narrow and provincial
views of life with God. God moments are meant to move our senses, and if we
rely on them to define normative faith experiences, the result may be a faith
void of moral and ethical accountability.

The God moment I experienced in my den left me with feelings of seren-
ity and closeness to God, but it didn't move me to think about how to help
my neighbor who had recently lost his job or the child across the street who
was born with severe disabilities. My God moment was all about me and what
I was feeling, and had a way of greatly reducing the size of my world where
others became only an afterthought.

Sacred Stories are different. They encompass an extensive framework
of ethical and moral concern that promotes putting others before ourselves.
The Golden Rule, a core value in Sacred Stories, teaches that we have responsibilities to our neighbor, and confirms that we are our brother's and sister's
keeper. These foundational faith narratives guide us in how we are to become

more engaged in I-Thou relationships by treating all people with respect and dignity.

Third, because God moments stress emotions of the heart, they reveal limited aspects about God's character, usually focusing on God's love. To know that God loves us is incredibly reassuring, and some might even suggest that God's love is the only thing of importance. The theologian Karl Barth, when asked what was the most significant truth he had learned in his theological studies, replied, "Jesus loves me this I know for the Bible tells me so." How wonderfully comforting to affirm that this one truth stands above all others in Scripture, but God's love is not one-dimensional. It needs to be defined and practically applied. What does it mean to be loved by God? How does God's love impact our interactions with others? How does God's love shape the way I live my life? Because God moments seldom offer a complete picture of God's character, they can result in a self-serving understanding of faith.

Sacred Stories paint a much larger canvas of God. For instance, Sacred Stories show God's love to be multi-dimensional. Not only does divine love comfort us, but God's love also makes demands on us. God's love, according to the Sacred Stories, is not a blank check that underwrites our selfish ambitions, but rather calls us to accept responsibility for our actions and to unselfishly love others. While God's love may be unconditional, there are clear conditions placed upon us once we open our hearts to receive it.

Fourth, God moments are seldom intended to be critically reviewed by others. God moments are private affairs of the heart and are not intended to be objects of debate, discussion, and disagreement. Those who have experienced God moments know that these special acts of grace are not meant to be thrown into the public arena for validation. In fact, doing so might rob them of their perceived meaning as God moments are not necessarily rational or even theological standards of faith. They are valuable because they offer comfort and consolation, and regardless of what other people think, we cherish these feelings as private expressions of God's grace.

Sacred Stories, on the other hand, are intended to be evaluated, scrutinized, and subjected to debate and discussion among not only people of faith, but also those who may be spiritually curious but have not yet taken the step of faith. Unlike God moments Sacred Stories are not private matters of the heart, but represent experiences we have all struggled with and questioned, regardless of our religious leanings. Over generations these experiences with God grew in importance and were recognized as being pivotal to what it means to live life with God. They addressed perplexing issues in ways which resonated with people who had come to the end of their rope and were searching for hope beyond themselves. Gradually communities of faith confirmed that these stories, based on their universal message, moral and ethical influence, and reliable guidance, deserved to be guiding lights for both Israel and the church.

While there are many Sacred Stories in Scripture, the Exodus from Egypt and the Easter experience represent cornerstones for the Judeo-Christian faith. These Sacred Stories transcend God moments in every way described above. They remind us that God does not forget the lowly, the disenfranchised, the sick, the sinner, those who have lost all hope or even the dead.

THE EXODUS

For 400 years the people of Israel lived in bondage under the unremitting whip of their Egyptian masters. It is hard for us to even imagine what their lives must have been like. Isabel Wilkerson's brilliant book *Caste* describes in graphic detail the harsh day-to-day realities of slavery in eighteenth and nineteenth century America. Her depictions are gut-wrenching, but reading about slavery and experiencing firsthand its dehumanizing effects are two completely different things. Only those who have suffered through such evil and inhumane treatment can fully understand.

Israel understands. Century after century they cried out to God for deliverance, but no deliverance came. Babies were born into slavery, and those who survived childhood entered into forced labor where they lived short, pain-filled lives and died from exhaustion, abuse, and disease. Generation after generation knew only suffering and humiliation.

How did these enslaved people keep from drowning in a sea of despair? Why did they continue calling on a God who apparently had abandoned them?

Perhaps part of the answer lies in Israel's past, specifically the stories that had been handed down by their ancestors from one generation to the next. At night around campfires and while working in the heat of the day, they told stories of the great figures of old who had also experienced hardship and suffering. The first couple, Adam and Eve, knew what it felt like to lose Paradise. Abraham, Isaac, Jacob, and Joseph were well acquainted with dark and seemingly hopeless times. Sarah and Rebekah knew feelings of spiritual despair too. Each of these great patriarchs and matriarchs had vacillated between faith and doubt and had questioned the providential care of God. Their stories were often messy, filled with both honorable and dishonorable behavior. They were human beings, creatures of flesh and blood, subject to the same human weaknesses as are we all. They struggled with understanding the ways of God and sometimes scratched their heads in frustration at God's unpredictable nature.

But these Sacred Stories reminded the enslaved Israelites that God had made a promise that all the nations of the earth would be blessed through this tiny, seemingly insignificant people (Gen. 12:3). That promise fueled Israel with passion and purpose that their existence was a sign of hope for all people. The remembrance of their purpose brightened their darkest days and made bearable their most severe trials. Without believing in their destiny they would have given in to hopelessness.

Life with God can be particularly exasperating. In the modern world we don't have much patience with God, and we wonder why God remains silent and why God doesn't act in a more decisive way to rectify the ills of our sick world. We often feel overwhelmed by our illnesses, disabilities, and disappointments without end and feel powerless to change the course of our lives. Where can we find some meaning to life when much of it appears so meaningless?

Theologians have a myriad of theories to explain why life is so cruelly unfair—maybe pain and suffering are meant to somehow help us mature and grow into better human beings or maybe our difficulties are due to unrepentant sin or maybe heaven will more than compensate us for today's heartache. The fact of the matter is that no explanation completely satisfies our frustration as to why God doesn't intervene to ease the inexplicable misery that so many experience.

Abstract theories offer cold comfort for those who suffer, for those exiled to the dark shadow of faith, and that's where Sacred Stories can provide tangible relief, anchors of hope we can hold on to. The stories tell of others who have suffered, who have traveled through tumultuous storms, who doubted and questioned their faith, and who raised their voices in protest at the injustices of the world. These heroes of faith understand what we are going through and walk with us as we struggle to cope with our prisons of pain, whether they be emotional, physical or spiritual. Israel found strength in those Sacred Stories and so can we.

There may have been times when Israel questioned why God wasn't more directly involved in their plight, but even when God appeared distant and aloof, they drew encouragement and hope from the stories. As they told and retold the Sacred Stories in their homes, places of worship and in the daily grind of labor, they experienced the mysterious presence of God. To be sure, it was an indirect experience, and it required hearts of faith to perceive God, but Israel discovered that even when God seemed far, far away, there dwelt among them a divine presence in the telling of their Sacred Stories. Israel didn't gloss over her dire circumstances. These ancient tales were not illusions of fantasy. They were well aware of their fragile place in the world, but the stories threw out a lifeline of hope by connecting them to others who had also suffered, and not just persevered, but had overcome the temptation to turn their backs on God.

Israel's story did not end in Egypt. Her chains of bondage would eventually be broken and, through the leadership of Moses, she would discover a new future, a future of promise and hope. Israel's deliverance from Egypt stands as the singular event that would forever shape Israel's understanding of her role in history. The telling and retelling of this story became the centerpiece of Israel's faith. From the call of Moses, to the miraculous wonders in Egypt, to the parting of the sea, to God's protective hand in the wilderness, Israel would forever remember God's faithfulness. The story would be embraced by future generations as their story, a story they would relive together again and again. As Jon Levenson writes, "Telling the story brings it alive. . .'Each man is obligated to see himself as if he came out of Egypt.'" [1] Through the remarkable power of this Sacred Story people who lived hundreds or even thousands of years later could experience it afresh, and, by once again experiencing the story, hope would never be far away.

The Exodus story can be our Sacred Story too. It is not something we just read about in the Bible but is a story we can incorporate into our lives as living history, and one that we can experience through the mystery of faith. To view narratives like the Exodus from only a historical perspective impoverishes our faith. The Exodus reminds us that God never abandons the weak, the marginalized, and those who ask for help. Oceans of suffering are never so deep, so dark, that we are left to navigate alone.

EASTER

The other half of the biblical cornerstone of faith is the Sacred Story of Easter. The apostle Paul recognized Easter as the core tenet of the Christian faith (1 Cor. 15:17), for without Easter there would be no New Testament or church. Just as Judaism subscribes to the miracle of the Exodus for its existence, the Christian faith acknowledges the miracle of the resurrected Jesus as its starting point. Plainly, then, both religions trace their origins to a supernatural act.

Death is the inevitable conclusion of life. Every one of us will die. In some ancient religions, such as that practiced by the Egyptians, only the rich and powerful were rewarded with life after death. The resurrection of Jesus, however, democratizes the grave. Regardless of social status or race or even worthiness, the Easter story announces that death does not put a period to our story. Whatever happened on that first Easter morning remains a mystery, but the early followers of Jesus drew inspiration and hope from the resurrected presence of Jesus. In the morning light of Easter, the door to eternal life with God was thrown wide open.

But there was more. It was not just the defeat of death that ushered in a new era of hope, as wonderful as that was, but the complete reprogramming of the religious order. The inclusion of the disenfranchised, the religiously unclean, the sick, the poor, and the sinful into the family of God reversed traditional orthodoxy. The heretofore unacceptable and marginalized now have standing before God. While the God of the Old Testament had always been on the side of the poor, the ostracized and the underdog, the religious establishment often ignored or, even worse, rejected these categories of people as worthy of God's acceptance.

By the time of Jesus certain branches of Judaism had developed a belief in the resurrection of the dead, but, according to the traditional thought of the day, only the righteous would inherit everlasting life. Sinners, such people as tax collectors, prostitutes, lepers and the like, would spend eternity in a place of torment. Even the poor, the blind, and the sick were viewed with suspicion. There were a multitude of passages in the Bible that suggested that poverty resulted from disobedience or sloth, and it was thought that sickness was sent by God as punishment for sin. Conversely, prosperity and good health were signs of God's blessing.

The Easter message turned all of that thinking on its head. God does not favor the righteous above the unrighteous but extends divine love and presence to everyone. Sinners are as welcomed in God's house as are the righteous. If the Easter hope had remained buried, the revolutionary teachings of Jesus would have lacked credibility, but what the disciples experienced on Easter morning empowered the remembered words of Jesus with divine authority.

Unfortunately, many of the superstitions and misunderstandings of

Scripture perpetuated by religious tradition prevail even today among people of faith. A friend of mine diagnosed with cancer shared with me how some of his friends were reluctant to physically embrace him or stay in the same room. On more than one occasion I have listened to conversations by the well-to-do within the faith community speak of the less fortunate in derogatory terms, as if their poverty were somehow their fault. Jesus challenged all that. Both his defeat of death as well as his inclusionary and revolutionary teaching introduced a new religious paradigm. Instead of the traditionally ubiquitous, "Where God is, there is no suffering," Jesus shocked our religious prejudices by revealing in his own life, "Where suffering exists, there God is." Suffering and death and a host of other ills are still part of our world, but we no longer need to feel shame that we in the shadow have been rejected by God.

The Easter Sacred Story forever altered the way we think about God. While Jesus didn't explain why there is so much cruelty in our world, he did tell us that during troubling times God has not forgotten us. When our world flies apart, when our pain becomes unbearable, when we welcome death as a friend, there still is hope.

Generations long past have felt what we feel, have suffered as we suffer, have struggled with faith much like we struggle. But then they heard the Sacred Stories. They read, absorbed, and analyzed the Sacred Stories. They talked about the stories with their family, friends, and neighbors; they chronicled the stories into their history and called upon their transformative power during desperate times. The Sacred Stories inspire hope. The stories change lives.

The stories were not idle tales, wishful fantasies, for desperate sufferers or credulous worshippers. They possess an unexplainable, even unimpeachable core of truth. The stories defy the way the world normally works, but their historical effects cannot be denied. They gave birth to a deeper reality that God, while elusive and hidden, is nevertheless mysteriously present in our world.

SACRED STORIES GIVE MEANING TO LIFE

Sometimes when I am hiking on a mountain trail I may pull a chocolate bar out of my coat pocket and munch on it to boost my sugar level, providing me with a quick but temporary burst of energy. God moments serve a similar purpose in the life of faith. They fill an immediate need for comfort and assurance, but for the times when God's presence seems distant or even non-existent, we need more substantive support. Sacred Stories meet that need. They offer reliable sustenance for the long and arduous journey of faith.

We in the shadow read the story of the Exodus and clasp hands across the centuries with our spiritual forebears who often felt as lonely and spiritually isolated as we do. We grasp for some thread of hope and then, well, then we read the stories, stories that stay with us, that encourage us and speak to us. The teaching of Jesus coupled with the empty tomb tell us that hope may begin in a graveyard. When we read about Abraham struggling with obedience or the psalmist crying out to God in anguish or the distraught Job sitting on an ash heap, we are privileged to share community with them.

Somehow these stories of life and faith meet us where we are—in the midst of our tragedies, sufferings, and feelings of abandonment. We read these ancient stories and recognize ourselves in the script, and that is why they are called Sacred Stories. They have the power to introduce us to a new reality, a reality that enlarges our understanding of God, others and ourselves. The stories embolden faith; they grow dear to us and open a window to what our eyes could not see before, a vision where God is mysteriously present, even when our feelings suggest otherwise. In this new way of seeing the world, hope is so very near.

THE POWER OF STORIES

One day I was having lunch with a group of pastors and the topic of story came up—whether stories were effective tools in the presentation of biblical truths. One of my pastor friends shared that several of his parishioners didn't like for him to use stories in the pulpit. These members felt that stories weakened or even diluted the effectiveness of the Gospel. In their opinion story had the connotation of something that wasn't true.

In today's highly technological and scientific culture I suppose there are those who doubt the usefulness of stories. The word does carry some baggage. My mother would often use the noun "story" as a verb, "Don't you story to me!" she would scold, when I came home late and gave her some lame excuse. Other people associate story with fable or fairy tale. So I understand why in today's culture story has fallen under a cloud of suspicion.

But, on the other hand, I'm not sure we can explain great and profound truths without using story. Jesus told stories or parables throughout his ministry. Matthew goes so far as to say that Jesus never taught without sharing a story (Matt. 13:34). Stories have a way of drawing us into their world; they tug not only on our emotional strings but also touch our cognitive powers. Stories draw pictures of reality that help us to have a clearer understanding of the world on multiple levels. We have all shed tears when a story opened up our heart and caused us to see what we could not see before. Even scientists construct imaginative stories that lead to theories that in turn lead to new discoveries. Stories have power.

Fred Craddock, a captivating storyteller, tells the story of how the acclaimed writer Scott Momaday learned of his Indian heritage.[2] One early morning before the sun rose his father awakened him, helped him dress, and then drove him to the home of an old Indian squaw. Scott, just a small boy, was left with the woman for the remainder of the day.

The aged woman shared with Scott the story of his ancestors. She went far back in time and told stories of ancient tribal legends, religious rituals, fierce and courageous warriors. She emphasized that Scott was part of the great nation of people called Kiowa. The Kiowa were a proud and honorable nation, brave and fearless in battle but also fair-minded and benevolent in times of peace.

With words she painted pictures of the great buffalo hunts and the religious celebrations that followed. She described harsh winters where women and children froze to death. She chanted songs commemorating their famous victories and mourned the braves who were lost in battle. She wept as she told of the coming of the white man and the ensuing changes that gradually took place. When she described how the Kiowa people were removed to a reservation and deprived of their ancestral habitat, she bowed her head in sorrow.

The Indian boy was mesmerized by the stories and felt as if in some strange way he had been pulled into his ancestors' world. He felt his heart swell with pride as he began to understand who he was. For the first time he realized he was more than Scott Momaday; he was Scott Momaday, Kiowa Indian.

In the evening Scott's father picked him up and they drove home together. As Scott looked out of the car window, he knew that his life had forever changed. He now knew where he came from and who he was. He knew his story and knowing his story would shape the rest of his life.

When the Sacred Stories become our own, we are able to see a little more clearly into our past and discover that we are not alone. We learn that there are others who have walked this path before us and their experiences are not all that different from ours, and by embracing the Sacred Stories, our lives become intertwined with theirs. The Sacred Stories also illuminate the darker regions of faith to help orient us and give direction. We join Abraham on his way to Mount Moriah, we tread through the desert with Moses, we put our arms around the psalmists as they mourn the absence of God, and we walk with Jesus through the streets of Jerusalem on his way to Golgotha. These Sacred Stories shine brightly, providing beams of light in what sometimes can be a rather dark and discouraging world.

One of the oldest, if not the oldest, Sacred Stories in Scripture is found in Deuteronomy 26:5-10. This ancient creed of faith was passed down orally from one generation to another before it was finally written down. The first line reads: "A wandering Aramean was my ancestor"(NSRV). This ancient saying preserves the memory of what life was like before God. The Hebrew word "wandering" can be translated "at a loss" or "without direction" or even "aimless." The Sacred Story reminds us that before Abraham began his journey with God his life was aimless, without direction, and without hope. He wandered from one place to another and lacked orientation and purpose. But then, God. Abraham in some deeply mysterious way experienced God and his life was changed forever. Now he had a future, now he had hope.

I identify with my distant faith relative, Abraham. I know what it's like to be a rudderless ship tossed to and fro by the wind—without direction or purpose, feeling spiritually alone and empty. Maybe you've been there, too. Maybe you're there now. And maybe, just maybe, Sacred Stories can help you find your way.

CHAPTER 11

WHEN PROFANE WORDS BECOME WORDS OF PRAYER

The curse of a godless man can
sound more pleasant in God's ears
than the Hallelujah of the pious.

- Luther

I saw Linda for the first time during high school. I watched her as she awkwardly wobbled her way down the hallways of our school. Linda had muscular dystrophy and everything she did required a herculean effort. She labored to walk, to speak, to eat, even to breathe was an arduous task. The daily routines that most of us take for granted, things like picking up a fork or sitting down in a chair, exhausted Linda. Linda's genetic disorder would grow steadily worse throughout high school, robbing her of physical movement, speech, the ability to carry out the simplest of tasks, and eventually would kill her a few years after she graduated from high school.

My desk just happened to be next to Linda's in several classes during my junior and senior years, and we became casual friends. Mostly, we just smiled at each other, and occasionally we chatted about some trivial matter, nothing of importance. Linda had a hard time being understood, and that made an extended conversation extremely difficult.

When the bell rang and class was dismissed, I would pick up my books and hurry off to the next class. I said a quick goodbye and Linda disappeared from my life. I was a sixteen-year-old teenager, full of life, fun, and myself, and had little understanding of crippling disabilities.

Linda never enjoyed a single day with the freedom to live a normal teenage life. She never went out on a date, never kissed a boy, never drove a car, never stayed up all night with girlfriends listening to music, never danced at the prom. The common joys of being young Linda either missed altogether or experienced in a much more limited way.

After high school I forgot all about Linda until one summer her mom called and asked if I could drop by their house and visit her. Apparently, she had deteriorated considerably since high school and was now bedridden, and her mom thought a visit from a former high school classmate might be of some encouragement. I drove over to Linda's house.

When I entered the front door there was a large hospital bed in the center of the living room. Linda appeared asleep, a tiny, almost translucent body covered by sheets. The flesh was stretched so tightly around her face, I did not recognize her. When her mother aroused her and she opened her eyes, the sockets appeared almost hollowed out, making her eyes seem unusually large. Linda uttered a few words I didn't understand so her mother bent over the bed, her ear only inches away from Linda's mouth, and translated the sounds for me. I touched Linda's arm and hand. They were cold. I smiled at her and tried to reassure her that everything would be fine.

My words were empty, inane, without meaning. I knew everything would not be fine, but I did not know what else to say. I didn't stay long, as Linda quickly grew tired and drifted off to sleep. I stood awkwardly for a few moments before Linda's mother, shifting my weight from one leg to the other. Finally, I said that I would visit again soon and left the house.

Outside, I climbed back into my Volkswagen, put the key in the ignition and then fixated on the mimosa tree in the front yard. Linda would soon die. She would leave this earth without ever having experienced so many of the teenage joys that I took for granted. For the first time I realized how terribly unfair her brief existence had been.

I visited Linda a few more times that summer before she passed away, but I don't think she was ever aware of my presence after that first visit. There was a short obituary in the Daily Oklahoman that I cut out and saved for a while, but I eventually lost the clipping. Yet I have never forgotten Linda. Almost fifty years have passed, but I still remember the girl who wobbled down the hallways, whose life was so incredibly more difficult than mine.

Linda is just one of millions upon millions of people whose existence on this tiny planet knows little joy and happiness but lives in the shadow of misery and sorrow. Maybe, in fact, she was one of the lucky ones. Linda had a supportive and loving family who cared for her throughout her life. When she died she was surrounded by loved ones. Countless other tragic victims of nature's throwing of the genetic dice live without love, support or even a trace of hope. What life they have is often wretched and lonely and when they die there is no one to mourn.

The reality that myriads of human beings are born with crippling disabilities and diseases or suffer in unimaginable living conditions and are never given a fair shot at life calls into serious question not only the personal nature of God but whether God even exists. If God lived on earth, so goes a Yiddish saying, people would throw rocks at his window. That sentiment describes precisely how I have felt at times when I contemplate the appalling reality that so many are condemned to live.

As a pastor I have witnessed the effects of intense suffering as it slowly and mercilessly destroyed both the patient and family. I have left the ICU room of a dying six-year-old girl and hurried to my car, where I angrily vented my frustration at the way the world works. I've stood in a hospice room by the bedside of a once beautiful young wife, whose body had been savagely attacked by cancer, and found that the only comfort I could give to the grieving husband, who stood helplessly beside her, was to weep with him. In moments like these I struggle to find any tender feelings toward God.

I brood over the countless people who live in squalor, disease, and death, and when someone tries to tell me about how God watches over each of us and protects us from evil the words seem, if not empty of meaning, certainly thoughtlessly spoken. Too many people through no fault of their own spend their entire lives imprisoned in cells of pain and suffering, existing from one miserable day to the next with little hope of escape. However God watches over and protects us, it does not spare us from the ravages of life. Yes, God may be aware when a sparrow falls to the ground, but the fact is. . . sparrows keep falling to the ground.

It is not unreasonable for people of faith to assume that life with God will not be all smooth sailing, but there is hope, perhaps a shaky hope at best, that what storms we do experience will only be temporary. Be patient, we tell ourselves, only a little longer and the gray and dreary days will give way to clear skies, and God will once again favor us with blessing. The wait, however, can be interminable.

John Claypool, a once prominent pastor, was devastated when his second grade daughter Laura Lue was diagnosed with acute leukemia. During a particularly difficult time in the hospital Laura Lue's pain became almost unbearable. She asked her father, who stood an agonizing vigil beside her bed, if he had prayed to God to take away her pain. He assured her that he had prayed many times for God to heal her. The little girl softly whispered, "What did he say? When did he say it would go away?" Looking at his terminally ill child Claypool had to admit that God had not said a word. Heaven's response to Claypool's prayers had been silence.[1] The unrelenting pain continued and only in death did it finally release its grip.

Sometimes the dark skies do not clear. Pain and suffering, heartache and disappointment become permanent fixtures. People living with protracted misery of one form or another know only the shadow side of life. The hopeful presence of God appears nowhere in sight. How do we continue to place faith in a personal and loving God when our pain intensifies unabated and prayers fall on seemingly deaf ears?

There are multitudes of people who will never know much happiness or hope in this world. Their entire lives will be weighed down by hunger, fear, loneliness or disease, and any escape is found only in death. As depressing as this sounds, the reality that countless people, both young and old, live mostly in the shadow remains all too true. People living in war-torn places like Ukraine or children born in poverty-stricken areas in Liberia or Burundi or in some places of the United States know few days without deprivation or suffering. A walk through a children's hospital such as St. Jude or Schriners can open our eyes to life's brutal truths. While treatment for children with catastrophic illnesses has greatly improved, still, too many children know only days of suffering. And just think what kind of life crippled and disabled children experienced just fifty or sixty years ago before advances in medicine. Life can be terribly twisted. Carlyle Marney, a maverick Baptist minister of a generation ago, once confessed that God had a lot of explaining to do.[2] I agree. God, indeed, has a lot of explaining to do.

CONFRONTING GOD

In the church I attended as a teen I often heard it said by the teachers in our Youth Department that we must not question God. I was told that faith in God called for submission to God's plan for our lives, and whatever happened was, of course, God's plan. I was counseled, "Maybe we don't understand it now, but sooner or later God will make his perfect will for our lives clear, if only we would continue to trust him." Such religious passivity does much harm to young minds, for it not only distorts how people in the Bible responded to suffering, it leads to an erosion of faith in any thinking person. If God cannot be questioned about inexplicable tragedies, then God must be terribly insecure. Who would want to worship a Being who refuses to be questioned about life's beastly tragedies? If we ignore the tough questions of faith then, as Christian psychologist Richard Beck warns, "We can begin to suspect that the Bible is being used or deployed to achieve emotional and existential consolation."[3] If consolation, a form of escapism from life's inequities, is the only reason for religious belief, then religion loses its appeal for millions of people who yearn for a faith that is authentically honest and challenges them to reflect God's image by being people of love, compassion and grace.

The biblical writers, however, were not interested in trying to defend God's honor while sacrificing faith's integrity. Recognizing the importance of holding God accountable, the Old Testament scholar James L. Crenshaw notices that from Israel's origin the Sacred Stories affirmed the right of people of faith to protest, dissent or complain about the injustices all around them.[4] Confronting God was a vital part of Israel's faith. That human beings could complain contributed to the very survival of Israel's faith experience. Without being able to voice dissent to what was happening in their lives, Israel's religion would have lost any resemblance of integrity and would have soon faded from history.[5] Israel was well aware of and alert to the harsh truths of human existence and was troubled by what it experienced. Significant and loud voices in Israel's religious experience did not give God a pass when it came to questions of divine justice.

In a sense the nation's communal suffering served to hold the faith of Israel together as the people found solidarity in being able to raise their ethical and moral objections to God concerning the unfairness of life. Complaints are found throughout Scripture, notably in the Psalms, Ecclesiastes, the prophets, and Job as well as several prayers of Jesus. True, we are not given definitive answers as to why there is unjust suffering, but we are allowed to ask, even to shout and scream our innermost feelings. This shadow side of life comprises numerous chapters in the Sacred Stories of both Israel and the church.

When I was diagnosed with embryonal cell carcinoma my faith was shaken to its core. My wife and I had two small children, minimal insurance, and meager financial resources. I was serving as pastor of a church in Oklahoma City, still developing my theology and totally shocked by what had befallen me. I tried to pray, but my thoughts were confused and disjointed. My heart was screaming at God, but I believed that I had to control my outward emotions, especially when church members called or visited me. I didn't want them to see how utterly human I felt, and how angry I was at God. For some reason I believed that pastors should be above such spiritually negative feelings. One of my well-meaning staff members came to visit me and before he left he prayed with me, thanking God that I had not allowed bitterness to get the best of me. I could barely endure his prayer, as I was a boiling inferno of rage ready to explode.

The night before a major surgery to remove around seventy-five lymph nodes along my spinal region, my wife and I were speaking to the surgeon when the telephone rang in my room. I picked up the receiver and heard the voice of a former professor who had been a mentor for many years. Someone had informed him of my condition and the impending surgery.

Immediately, invectives and curses spilled out into my ear as my mentor and former teacher verbally assaulted God. I was too stunned to speak. I listened to his ranting that went on for several minutes. Then silence. I thought the connection had been broken. Softly, he began to speak again, but his tone had completely changed. He said he would call back in a few days and then over the phone, this man who had cursed God only moments before, prayed for me. As I replaced the receiver, I thought to myself, "I have some really weird friends."

Later in the evening, when the surgeon had left, I shared with my wife the conversation with the seminary professor. She, too, was shocked. Both of us had been taught never to challenge God and certainly never to shout or curse at God. This was unfamiliar terrain for us.

When my wife left the hospital I remained alone in the semi-dark room, thinking about what my friend had said about God. So incredibly abusive were his words that over thirty years later just to think about them causes me unease. I replayed the conversation over and over again in my mind, and then I slowly began to understand. My former teacher and friend had provided me with an inexpressible gift. He had voiced all the intense feelings and emotions that were buried within me, but had not been allowed to surface for fear that I might offend God. I dared not pray because I knew that my words would be filled with vitriolic rage, and once I opened my mouth, God would be the target of my fury.

In a few hours I would undergo an eight-hour operation that would reveal whether my life would be cut short, but now I felt as though a weight had been lifted from my heart. What had been suppressed deep within me had been given free reign, liberating me from hiding a dark secret. Instead of feeling guilty or ashamed, I felt relief. A friend had cared enough about me to give voice to what he believed I could not or would not say on my own. His profane words became the holy words I could not bring myself to pray.

Over the next few years my faith took a significant turn as I began to realize that complaint, dissent, protest and other negative emotions are not abnormal expressions of faith but are characteristic of real faith. We are often cowed into thinking that God's feelings are easily ruffled, and dire consequences await us if we dare challenge God. Nothing could be further from the truth. Honest and authentic faith requires, no, demands, that our hearts and souls be allowed to vent our true feelings before God. Instead of retribution, we find understanding, comfort and grace. We live in a troubled world and life is unpredictable and often brutally tragic, and the privilege of crying out to the heavens "Why?" is not only our right, it is our responsibility as creatures fashioned in the image of God. The freedom to pour out our heart before God, even though what spills forth may be full of bitterness and anger, ironically, may become a channel for hope. By granting us the privilege to complain and voice our rage, faith gains credibility. The sufferings of so many in this world are incomprehensible, but if our faith encourages us to peel back the layers of our heart, exposing the raw wounds of pain, disappointment, and despair that throb within us, then, perhaps, healing can eventually take place. And with healing comes hope.

In the past few chapters we have looked at the Sacred Stories of Adam and Eve, Abraham, Moses and some of the psalmists, many of whom are anonymous. These figures stand out as pillars of faith, but their life with God was not always confident and filled with certitude. When read closely these stories reveal that these so-called model believers were often mired in the depths of doubt and despair. They knew feelings of hopelessness and abandonment, and despite the fact that these biblical characters are often celebrated by the church as examples of steadfast faith, the Bible makes clear that they were well acquainted with life in the shadow.

Israel and the early church clearly recognized that faith in a God who was present, attentive, and faithful presented significant challenges. In the Sacred Stories which represent their faith journeys, room was made for the testimonies of those who struggled with faith and for those who barely held on.

Surprisingly, these darker faith stories are scattered throughout the pages of the Bible. No doubt some in the faith community felt uncomfortable with such brazen attacks on the reliability and trustworthiness of God, nevertheless, the biblical witnesses believed it important to include these expressions of faith, even those that challenged the more emotionally satisfying stories of comfort and consolation.

HOLDING GOD ACCOUNTABLE

The Book of Psalms has often been called the hymn book or prayer book of ancient Israel. These deeply spiritual writings are prayers and songs that convey the life of faith for both joyous and distraught believers. How often troubled souls have turned to the psalms in times of crisis. Passages such as "The Lord is my Shepherd, I shall not want," or "Cast your burden on the Lord, and he will sustain you," or "God is our refuge and strength, a very present help in trouble" as well as many other verses have comforted and provided hope for individuals through the centuries. These passages display the joys of divine presence, but those in the shadow can also find solace in these tender yet powerful words.

There are, however, other psalms that sound more strident notes. More than half of the psalms reflect feelings of divine abandonment or divine indifference in times of peril. These psalms speak of life with God as unpredictable, even disappointing, and, on occasion, it seems as though God has abdicated God's covenant responsibilities. Complaint, dissent, and protest fill the pages of the psalter. If complaining to God were somehow off limits, then why do the psalms inhabit such a prominent place in Scripture? In this book valued for millennia by both Jews and Christians, the psalms give ample room to disgruntled, disillusioned, and spiritually hopeless people. These poetic voices speak of incoherent and disorienting times that seemingly, in some cases, never end. We have already looked at a few of these psalms that describe the various experiences of life with God, but a more indepth look at these frank confessions will give us a more complete picture of the shadowy side of faith that so many of us know all too well. The selected psalms represent only a sampling.

Psalm 13

Have you ever felt completely abandoned by God? When one pain-filled day follows another, feelings that God has left us can rob us of any sense of hope, and sometimes we don't even know why God has seemingly forgotten us.

It may give us some relief to know that we are not the only ones who have experienced God's withdrawal from our lives. Numerous psalmists also felt forsaken by divine presence and questioned why God had turned away from them. Psalm 13 is a prayer that many of us have prayed, maybe with different words but with the same sentiment.

> How long, O Lord?
> Will you forget me forever?
> How long will you hide your face from me?
> (Ps. 13:1 NRSV)

The psalmist mourns the absence of God in his life and does not know when God will favor him again. The writer pleads with God to answer him and restore the broken relationship. No reason is given for God's withdrawal. No mention is made of sin or an act of disloyalty on the part of the psalmist. The psalmist is burdened with sorrow, feels vulnerable to the threats around him and fears that his life is nearing an end (Ps. 13:2). The psalmist pleads for God to look upon him, to turn once again toward him that he may know divine blessings.

Why God withdraws divine presence from us is a mystery, but the effects of God's abandonment are very real. We not only feel alone, but we also feel betrayed.

Years ago I became friends with a man from the Rotary club named Bubba. Bubba was a fun-loving fellow with an infectious smile and a deep commitment to his Christian faith. I often sat at the table with him during Rotary meetings where we would visit about an assortment of subjects, but normally he would turn the conversation to God. Bubba expressed his faith in beautiful ways, always encouraging people and reminding them that he was only a phone call away.

I was grieved to hear at one of the Rotary meetings that Bubba had been diagnosed with inoperable bone cancer. Everyone in the club was visibly upset as Bubba had endeared himself to all of us, regardless of religious affiliation. I visited him several times in the hospital, but my last visit continues to trouble me.

He was in obvious pain from the cancer which had spread throughout his body, breaking several of his bones, and eroding others. Unable to reach out to me with his arms, and barely able to speak, he blinked repeatedly until I bent over his bed, my ear close to his mouth. His voice was a raspy whisper, barely audible, but I believe he said only one word, "Why?" I raised my head back up and looked at my friend. I didn't have an answer.

I don't know for sure what Bubba meant. But I think he wondered, like the psalmist, why God had seemingly forgotten him. At one time or another many of us have wondered too.

Some interpreters suggest the psalm concludes on a summery note. The psalmist pledges his trust in God's promised commitment, expressed by the Hebrew word "hesed," which signifies "abiding love," and proclaims that in spite of his present difficulties, God has been good to him (Ps. 13:5). Verses five and six are open to wide interpretation. Some scholars suggest the threat has passed and now the psalmist prays his gratitude to God. Meanwhile, other theologians think that praise and complaint are symbiotically related and represent a more holistic expression of faith, something akin to suffering only lasts a season and then there is assured blessing. Maybe. Then, too, the last two verses conceivably could be understood as wishful thinking on the part of the writer. By projecting a confidence in God, perhaps more contrived than felt, the psalmist may have been trying to force God's hand, putting God on the spot by reminding God of the promises of old. This interpretation hardly represents a ringing endorsement of God—more like a desperate attempt to arouse God to do something! Desperate times, though, call for desperate measures, and there will come a time in our prolonged suffering when we will say or do anything to ease our pain, even if it means a feeble attempt at trying to cajole God.

Psalm 88

Those who dwell in the regions where calm seas are the normal faith experience find it almost impossible to identify with those battered by enduring storms of disappointment and disillusionment. If God is distant, there must be some reason, some explanation, why. It is human nature to assess blame on those who perpetually suffer. The writer Simone Weil writes that everybody "despises the afflicted to some extent, although practically no one is conscious of it."[6] It is inconceivable for many in the faith community that God would inflict God's wrath upon innocent victims. We bolster our faith by insisting that if there are people who live primarily in the realm of suffering, they must have done something to offend God, some sin for which they deserve punishment.

And yet, there are voices in Scripture that call into question God's fairness, and these voices speak for many who can't understand why life is so savagely cruel, why prayers go unanswered, why suffering never abates. Psalm 88 is one such voice. The psalm voices the prayer of a person who knew nothing but suffering his entire life, apparently, through no fault of his own. If he has sinned, he makes no attempt to confess it or ask forgiveness. He lives in an endless circle of pain from which there is no way out. It is one of the most tragic and heart-wrenching chapters in Scripture. That this prayer found a place in the Bible tells us that Israel did not try to smooth over the jagged and irreconcilable contradictions of faith but believed that in some way these complaints were authentic confessions of life with God.

The psalmist begs God again and again to listen to him, to relieve him of his suffering but to no avail. Every day he calls upon God but his prayers seemingly never reach the ears of God (Ps. 88:9). Not only does God not listen, but the psalmist blames God for his miserable condition: "I suffer your terrors; I am desperate. Your wrath has swept over me; your dread assaults destroy me" (Ps. 88:15-16 NRSV). When unexplained suffering forces us to our knees, we look for someone to hold responsible, even if it's God. So dire is the situation that the psalmist believes even his friends have turned their backs on him (Ps. 88: 8, 18). He has been forsaken by both God and friends and feels completely alone. He closes his prayer by saying his only companion is darkness. The psalmist feels trapped and alone in his misery, with no possible way out.

What I find remarkable about this psalm is that the one praying still bothers to pray! Still believes! Still has hope! He longs for God even though his prayers are unanswered, even though God remains an inaccessible mystery. He cannot and will not abandon God. The Catholic theologian Karl Rahner speaks for many in the shadow when he writes that those "who pray and receive the sacraments, nevertheless find themselves at home in a wintry sort of spirituality, in which they stand alongside the atheist, but obviously without becoming atheists themselves."[7] How eerie and humbling and true that in the life of faith both belief and unbelief are so closely linked.

We may wonder why this gloomy prayer is even in the Bible. It certainly has a different tone than, say, Psalm 23, everyone's favorite. And, yet, when we find ourselves in inexplicable dungeons of pain and suffering, when every day our prayers for help go unanswered, we may find that Psalm 88 is exactly the place to turn. At first the psalm may strike us as the one place not to go.

After all, the prayer doesn't give much evidence of hope. So why should we read this rather pessimistic psalm of darkness?

First, the prayer reflects how many of us have prayed at one time or another. Whether we have verbalized the words, most of us can identify with the emotion. Haven't there been times when you felt that God had let you down? Haven't you known days when you felt completely abandoned by both God and friends? By sharing his faith journey and by telling us how he feels, the psalmist enters into our world, not as a stranger but as a soulmate. He voices some of our own frustrations with God and by so doing empathizes with us and becomes a source of support.

Then, too, the psalmist continues to engage with God. He has every reason to call it quits, to renounce his faith. Many in similar circumstances would have thrown in the towel, and we would sympathize with them, but the psalmist doesn't give up on God and his tenacity may serve to guide us when the bottom falls out. When we find ourselves in the valleys of faith, when all around us there is darkness and despair, when suffering defines our existence, we might be tempted to turn our backs on God, but then we read this prayer by a man who suffered immensely but never gave up on God.

In my own life of faith I have grown so frustrated that in my darkest moments I have contemplated life without God. But then, where else might I turn? What other options are there, if not God? No satisfactory alternative remotely comes close to the possibility of God. I weigh the options but at the end of the day I am persuaded that God's reality may not always be felt but that doesn't mean that divine presence has abandoned me. God's presence may not be a way out of darkness but a way to live in the midst of darkness. So like the psalmist, I continue to pray, sometimes venting my feelings of spiritual disgust and disappointment, but all the while I pray—just like the psalmist.

The psalmist ends his prayer by claiming his only companion is darkness. I understand that sometimes our pain, sadly, blinds us from seeing any light and we miss the countless friends and fellow-sufferers who stand with us. In the darkness we may not see them, but they are there. Job, for instance, knows what the psalmist is feeling. Job is there with him. Jeremiah is there, too. He understands exactly what it is like to be abandoned by God. And Abraham has walked in the same shadow as the psalmist. He, too, knows all about dark times. There are countless other men and women who identify with the psalmist. He is not alone and neither are we.

When misery and feelings of hopelessness come barreling into our lives, it is quite natural to feel bereft of companions. We watch others as they enjoy lives filled with blessing, while we experience nothing but sorrow and heartbreak, but it is important to remember that in the darkness we are never without companions. If we will move toward others in I-Thou relationships, we will discover that they are also moving toward us, not in judgement but in human tenderness, and by opening our lives to other people through acts of love, compassion, and understanding, we may discover that God is not so very far away after all.

Like most ministers I have had my share of conversations with atheists. Sometimes the person sitting across from me is merely sowing his intellectual wild oats, trying to impress or startle me with his newly acquired philosophical knowledge. On occasion, however, I have had deep and meaningful exchanges with people who sincerely were searching for some evidence of God but just couldn't find it.

Earlier in my ministry I would try to overwhelm people who struggled with the God question with a barrage of finely tuned apologetics. Not anymore. God's love can't be proven by arguments. Only other people of flesh and blood can validate the presence of God. After a lifetime of listening to people in pain, seeing heartbreaking tragedies and an assortment of other ills, I have learned to sympathize with those who aren't able to negotiate the distance between unbelief and belief. It is a short distance, really, but I have found that it can only be traversed by acts of love.

Psalm 44

All too often we associate God's withdrawal from our lives with sin or disobedience. If God removes divine presence from us it is because we have sinned or betrayed God in some way. There are instances, however, when no explanation is given for God's absence. There are places in Scripture where God withdraws for no apparent reason. In Psalm 44:17-19, for instance, the psalmist believes that God has forsaken Israel without justification.

> *All this happened to us, though we had not forgotten you*
> *or been false to your covenant. Our hearts had not turned back;*
> *our feet had not strayed from your path. But you [God]*
> *crushed us and made us a haunt for jackals and covered*
> *us over with deep darkness.*
> *(NIV)*

The psalmist voiced a prayer on behalf of the people who were confused by God's abandonment and pleads with God to return (Ps. 44:23). The prayer contains no confession of sin, only a reminder to God that even though divine presence has withdrawn from them, God's people have remained faithful. One senses utter dismay when the psalmist tries to awaken God from his slumber:

> *Awake, O Lord! Why do you sleep?*
> *Rouse yourself! Do not reject us forever.*
> *Why do you hide your face and forget our misery and oppression?*
> *(NIV)*

How nearly impossible it is for us to comprehend the gravity of Israel's distress! We read these complaints and cries of sorrow far removed from Israel's anguish, much like a person who can no longer remember the days of painful recovery after a major surgery. For the person who is only a day or two post-op, however, the misery is all too real.

People suffering the full brunt of debilitating sorrow and loss read these passages with desperate hope. "Maybe there is someone who understands what I am going through." When we go through trauma of some kind it is natural to feel isolated and alone. We may feel as though no one else can truly comprehend, and we would be right. Every experience of suffering is unique. Yet, if we think that other people have gone through similar times, not identical but similar, and managed somehow to cope and survive, then maybe there is a way forward for us. Therein lies much of the value of the psalms. The psalms bequeath hope by voicing the prayers that we have been unable to pray because we have grown disillusioned, bitter, or perhaps, full of rage. Yet, by listening to the prayers of others, who have also known harrowing days, we may not feel so alone and hopeless. Their complaints may loosen our own tongues, giving us permission to confront God and empty our hearts of dark and suppressed feelings.

When we bask in the joy of God's presence, it is convenient to forget those who are caught in an unending nightmare. We turn our heads away when confronted with a tragic figure, perhaps because we know way down deep that we are only one step away from a similar fate. Some people of faith may be able to live above the suffering and pain where so much of humanity dwells, like a rock skipping across the water, but eventually the rock loses its momentum and sinks. And when you find yourself at the bottom, it is comforting to know that you are not alone. These psalms and many more like them were prayed by those who had sunk to the depths, and their words provide a chorus of encouragement and hope.[8]

ACKNOWLEDGING THE DARKNESS

The raw emotion of these psalms of despair are often emptied of their sharp sting by those who insist that these sorrowful and mournful pleas are in reality "preliminary to statements of confidence and praise" in God.[9] In other words, whatever misery we may experience in the life of faith is a mere momentary pause as good times are always just ahead. Whatever trage- dy you endure today will be offset by tomorrow's blessing. If we interpret the psalms in this way the testimonies of these beleaguered people have no value in and of themselves, but are merely precursors to blessing and pros- perity. Martin Marty understands the importance of identifying with these forlorn souls by adding that "not to see the world through the eyes of the victim, is to be cut off from humanity."[10] If we read the psalms as authentic expressions of those who suffer, then we are forced to stand with them and acknowledge their anguish because to move too quickly beyond the shadow into the light trivializes what they are going through.

Just after the 300,000th death from the coronavirus was recorded in the United States, a friend wrote to me that he was glad he had a heaven to look forward to. As a person of faith, I share his hope, but his timing startled me. Before we can speak of hope, it is important first to acknowledge the dark- ness of what has transpired. We must take time to try and absorb the shock of the hundreds of thousands of lives that have been lost. To speak too soon of the hope of eternal life minimizes the all-too-real tragedy of untimely death.

If our feelings of rejection and abandonment are just transient anomalies that only touch the surface of heartache but never really come to terms with its reality, then that would mean the wretchedness of existence is of little concern to God. Theologian Samuel Balentine understands that if our experi- ences of tragedy are only brief episodic events before assured blessing, then "the questions directed toward God [by the psalmists and all those who suf- fer] would be meaningless, and to interpret all questions merely preliminary to confessions of confidence is to be indifferent to the agony of the struggle out of which they were born."[11] If, however, the psalms of sorrow are reflec- tions of an authentic faith experience, then God must take them seriously as the heartfelt expressions of people living through the torturous seasons of faith. It is true that both praise and lament signify valid witnesses to life with God, but they are not bound to each other. Joy does not always follow mourning in the real world. There are prolonged periods in life when sorrow sucks all the oxygen out of the room and only emptiness and hopelessness remain. Grief may not always give way to joy.

WOUNDS THAT DO NOT HEAL

Clay was five or six years old when I became his pastor. He was a beautiful blond-haired boy with a quick smile and a charming and outgoing personality. Clay was cursed with cystic fibrosis, at that time a death sentence. In spite of his chronic health problems Clay was musically talented and often played the piano for the church. He touched my heart as few children have. His parents were well-to-do and tried every treatment to help their son, but his fate was inevitable.

When Clay passed away as a teenager, I had already left the church and moved to a neighboring state to assume a new pastorate. The parents, however, knowing my love for their son, called and asked me to return and perform the funeral service. Of course I agreed and boarded a plane a few days later to conduct the service for my young friend Clay.

The sanctuary was packed, mostly with young people from the high school where Clay attended. Both young and old were inconsolable, and the palpable grief in the room was overwhelming, as though a heavy blanket of gloom draped the audience.

Clay's death was no precursor to praise. His passing was tragic, and no amount of sermonizing could smooth over the jagged edges of the immense anguish Clay's parents and friends suffered through. We can speak of the resurrection hope and eternal life with God, and a person of faith does, but this hope does not attenuate the bitterness of unjust suffering and extreme premature death. To ignore or gloss over this cruel reality permits faith to serve as a kind of narcotic, numbing our senses from having to deal with the harshness of our present reality. The life of faith then becomes a form of escape, hardly a way of life worthy of beings created in the image of God.

Psalms of sadness and complaint, with their inherent feelings of divine rejection, cannot be smoothed over by promises of some future life in heaven. These Sacred Stories of a darker faith serve as a reminder of the fragility of our existence and the ambiguity associated with words like belief and unbelief.

When the bottom falls out, our first response may be to pretend that all is well, and we may even utter words expressing confidence in God. But when the days continually grow darker with no relief in sight and God seems far away, we will eventually raise our voice to the heavens and ask, "Why?" Why has God abandoned me? Why has my life taken this turn? Way down deep, the place where souls confess their innermost thoughts, bitterness and brokenness rage against the heavens; confusion, doubt, and hurt overwhelm the place where once faith stood steadfast and confident. In this world some wounds do not heal, even with time. Our faith may be bruised, battered, barely hanging on, or maybe we have slowly moved away from God altogether.

When the life of faith seems barren, when the shadow refuses to recede, we may feel as though God has a lot of explaining to do. The psalmists agree, and their Sacred Stories resonate with untold numbers of people who know more shadow than light in their life with God. If we accept the Bible as a reliable guide for the life of faith, then, mercifully, even our profanities may become words of prayer in the ears of God. Amen.

CHAPTER 12

YOU HAVE A
RIGHT TO BE HEARD

The very act of speaking in the midst of pain and suffering is an act of faith.
It signals fierce resolve to believe that someone will listen,
someone will care, someone will come.

- Samuel Balentine

Most of us have experienced feelings of disorientation when life spins out of control and craters after endless days of blessing. Sometimes our assured confidence in God can abruptly be lost, and, without warning, we can find ourselves languishing in the murky region between belief and unbelief. Such questions as, "Where is God when I need him?" "Why hasn't God answered my prayers?" "Why has God allowed this terrible tragedy to happen?" "Why hasn't God fulfilled his promise to watch over and protect me?" refuse to release their grip on us. And, of course, there are a thousand other unresolved issues that fill our hearts and minds as we wonder why God has seemingly left us in the lurch. As we have seen, the psalms raise similarly disturbing questions repeatedly as do the stories of the patriarchs and prophets. But these are not the only places in the Bible we see these questions.

The New Testament also reveals the disciples and Jesus struggling with the inexplicable ways of God. In addition, there are other books in the Bible that specifically focus on lesser-known faith experiences where God seemed distant or unapproachable, where God appeared to have abdicated responsibilities to do what was right and good.

While these disturbing faith stories are often ignored or only selectively read, they too reflect authentic descriptions of life with God. These troublesome faith experiences raise flags of warning to those enjoying a perpetually comfortable and predictable life with God that is often the standard model of faith in the contemporary church. So important was it for both Israel and the church to be true to their faith understanding, they refused to cover up or bypass these darker and more unsettling witnesses. It is as though the biblical writers want everyone to be fully informed, to know the truth about the inevitable shadow that sooner or later will darken everyone's life. The fact is, according to the Sacred Stories, life with God may be hazardous to your health.

SHADOWY PERSPECTIVES OF FAITH

Biblical writers as a rule didn't dabble in abstract philosophical thought. The faith of Israel and the church teaches a way of life that is practical and consumed with addressing the problems of everyday life. The narratives in the Old Testament and the lessons of the New Testament concentrate on how we are to live together in community as God's people.

There are a few biblical books, however, that inch toward the philosophical spectrum—Ecclesiastes and Job among them. These two writings question more traditional views of faith and consequently give a more dissonant picture of life with God. Pastors struggle to find uplifting sermon material from these works. The books present a sardonic, some would even argue a depressing view of life with only granular visions of hope. Their bleak perspectives do not hide frustration, bitterness, and anger directed toward God and boldly bear witness to some of the most troubling passages in all of Scripture. Yet, the experiences they describe are also Sacred Stories and to ignore them may prevent us from seeing a broader and more complete canvas of faith. We never know what lies ahead and by marginalizing these distressing faith stories, we may not be prepared for the discouraging days of life with God that are sure to come. But even within these darker stories, if you look closely, there are signs of hope.

ECCLESIASTES

The writer of Ecclesiastes is the closest thing to a philosopher we have in Scripture. He asks penetrating questions and suggests answers that border on heresy. He pushes faith in God to the edge and then lets it stand on the precipice, tottering back and forth. It is as though the writer intentionally wants to keep us off balance.

Ecclesiastes views the world with an unfiltered lens and in the end, throws up his hands in despair: "Everything is utterly, utterly absurd" (Eccl. 1:2). Given its depressing description of life, few people thought the book worthy of admission into Scripture, but influential rabbis recognized the Sacred Story in the writing and insisted it be included in the canon. Because the writer seeks to instruct how life is to be lived, the book is often referred to as "the Teacher." The Teacher is a rather pessimistic sage and sends a somber message that life is absurd or meaningless. This phrase is repeated throughout the book, leaving little or no room for optimism. This is definitely not a book for those seeking a feel-good religion.

We do not hear many sermons from Ecclesiastes, usually only from Eccl. 3:1-11—"For everything there is a season," made popular in the sixties by the Byrds' hit, Turn! Turn! Turn! The Teacher plants few morsels of optimism, finally settling on eating and drinking and enjoying one's work as the only meaningful course in life (Eccl. 2:24). Make the most of your time on earth, he tells us, for it will soon end! Not exactly the best advertisement for life with God!

The Teacher finds little about life that is praiseworthy. From his vantage point nothing really matters. Whether one lives a righteous life or a wicked life, the fate is the same—the grave, a place void of feeling, passion, and meaning. The Teacher hates life (Eccl. 2:17). It would have been better not to have been born (Eccl. 4:3). Yet, he does not advocate the premature ending of life. Life is to be lived to the fullest extent possible, for "even a live dog is better off than a dead lion!" (Eccl. 9:4 NIV). He extends virtually no comfort that might provide some ray of hope. He looks squarely into the face of the absurdity of existence and does not flinch. For the Teacher, according to biblical scholar Sibley Towner, "life [is] lived without self-deception, without despair, life [is] lived in full questioning awareness."[1] The only recourse in such a sad and dismal world, according to the Teacher, is to celebrate what life God has given us because the grave awaits us all.

Ecclesiastes could be the poster child for people of faith who long for greater clarity when it comes to divine presence, but see only the day to day reality of a world that seems to stagger along without an engaged Creator. We in the Shadow find theological kinship with the Teacher who has studied life around him, seen cruel injustices and unimaginable suffering, witnessed the innocent die with equal regularity as the guilty, and simply can't balance what he sees with the claims of many in the faith community who subscribe to an attentive and beneficent God. Like many of us, the Teacher doesn't go so far as to deny the existence of God, but he does question whether life with God makes any difference. At the end of the day, according to the Teacher, whether a person devotes himself to God or not, the end result is the same.

Ecclesiastes spells out in blunt terms that those who exercise faith in God should not expect any favors or advantages in this world. The same rules apply to those who live life with God as those who never darken the door of a sacred place or bow their knee in prayer. If people of faith expect some direct divine intervention when the going gets tough, they will likely be disappointed, as life appears to be driven more by chance than providence. The message of the Teacher is bleak, even depressing, but it is also a hard message to refute, and, at one time or another, many of us have felt the same sense of despair as the Teacher.

While there are plenty of people who would vigorously defend the principle of an ordered world and push back on the Teacher's so-called wisdom, there are others whose faith experience parallels that of the Teacher. We of this darker faith story identify with much of what the ancient skeptic has written and commiserate with the raw honesty of his Sacred Story. When we in the shadow hear of a faith experience like Ecclesiastes, we may think, "Aha! Here is someone who understands me and can identify with my faith experience. I can talk to this person; I can trust this person. I am no longer alone."

The Sacred Story in Ecclesiastes is not one that people of faith turn to for their morning devotional reading, especially those who know seemingly uninterrupted days of divine presence, but it is a necessary story that people of faith should read, in fact, must read, if there is to be any balance and authenticity in their faith journey. Too often, in order to make faith appealing, the church presents life with God as a kind of fairy-tale adventure, where good prevails over evil and the faithful live happily ever after. The Teacher, however, pushes back on this one-sided narrative, and his unvarnished and unedited view that life can be absurd calls into question the belief that God hovers over the lives of the faithful, ready to rescue any who meet with adversity, so long as they play by the rules.

The Teacher reminds me of a fascinating friend I knew in seminary who believed in and followed the ways of God, yet enjoyed playing the devil's advocate by challenging his more traditionally-minded classmates to think through their faith commitment. He had little patience with those entering the ministry who thoughtlessly submitted to religious dogma just because it had been handed down through the centuries. He pushed aspiring ministers to look within and question why they believed what they did, even if it caused a few animated ministerial squabbles in the seminary cafeteria from time to time.

He was viewed by many as a maverick, a trouble maker, someone who shouldn't even be in ministry, but I admired his thirst for truth and his refusal to swallow hook, line and sinker the prevailing theological winds of the day. He forced me to confront uncomfortable questions, such as why I chose a religious path. Did my fear of life's existential uncertainties, the reality of death and suffering, drive me into what I thought would be a more sheltered life, with its supposed order, predictability and assurance?

To a certain extent, yes, and it took me time to settle in my mind that my ministry path was not merely an attempt to escape from the world but was a way to engage the world by offering a more fulfilling vision of life. But there were other reasons, too, that I had never thought about until my friend's sharp probes forced me to honestly consider why I wanted to be a minister. For me the God question was life's ultimate mystery, and I felt drawn to a life that would be dedicated to this issue. Then, too, I also wanted to live a life that made a practical difference, to be present with people who faced the myriad of things that dehumanize existence, especially those who were condemned to live in the shadow of suffering and pain. My unorthodox friend helped me to clarify my reasons for ministry and made me a more conscientious person of faith.

When I read Ecclesiastes, I find within its pages a person who speaks for me and countless others who have made the decision to venture life with God but can't buy into the idea that God directly engages with the smallest detail of our lives. Yes, there are benefits in life with God, benefits that may not show up in our bank statements or spare us from getting cancer or save us from a tragic accident, but, just the same, there is a satisfaction, a sense of peace, that comes from trying to live as God's image in the world by doing what is right and good. When we treat others with respect and dignity, when we love and care for family and friends, when we live more simply so that the less fortunate may simply live, and when we welcome the stranger in our midst, we are building a better world, a world where there is less suffering, less heartache and where there is enough for everyone. To be sure, there is much absurdity in life, but if we strive to help improve the lives of others, then at least our time on earth will have been well spent. It may be the one way to instill a sense of meaning into a world of absurdities.

THE UNLUCKY ONES

Several times in Ecclesiastes the word "sinner" occurs (Eccl. 2:26: 9:18 NIV). The Hebrew word for sinner, *hote*, can also mean "fool," or "bungler" or even "unlucky one." The Teacher has a deterministic attitude concerning life, that is, all life is predetermined. There are some who are fortunate and blessed, while others are unfortunate and cursed, or so it seems. According to the Teacher, the cursed ones, the people who are unlucky in health or business or who are born to the wrong parents or happen to reside on the wrong side of the tracks are simply out of luck. He offers no condolences to these unfortunate people; in the ancient world of Israel the unlucky ones are simply "sinners," those stricken by the precarious nature of a world gone amok.

The Teacher's perspective would be challenged by Jesus (John 9:2), who held that the unlucky ones are not guilty of greater sin than the lucky ones, and they certainly have not been rejected by God. The "Good News" of the New Testament announces that the unlucky ones of this world have been embraced by God.

Jesus challenges the so-called "lucky ones," those who have been fortunate in this world, to provide a helping hand to the unlucky ones. Throughout the New Testament there is a heavy emphasis on social justice. The Bible rejects a philosophy of life that seeks to increase one's own materiality while the less fortunate go without. Because all human beings are created in the image of God no single human being is less deserving than another. Both the Talmud and the Qur'an affirm that to save a single life is as though one has saved the entire world. While both religions may only be referring to fellow Jews or Muslims, it doesn't require much soul-searching to realize the expression transcends partisan religion. And the teachings of Jesus clearly underscore this universal moral truth.

ECCLESIASTES: ONE SACRED STORY AMONG MANY

The Teacher describes a faith experience that is dark, somewhat depressing. Still, while much in the book is disturbing, I have also found refreshing truths in the words of this ancient sage and even traces of hope. Life sometimes makes no sense. Haven't we all felt the Teacher's despair? Haven't we all known periods when life felt absurd? When I return from the hospital where a teenager has just died from a brain tumor or hear on the radio of a natural disaster or learn of any number of unexplained tragedies, I find myself agreeing with the Teacher—life can be ridiculous and there appears to be at times no meaning to our existence. To whitewash these feelings would be to turn our backs on our humanity, and to ignore our humanity robs faith of credibility. Life with God is not a way to avoid life's problems; it is a way to face life's cruel realities—together.

Ecclesiastes is one Sacred Story in the biblical diary of faith, but there are many other Sacred Stories as well. The Teacher reminds me to live my life to the fullest, to make every day count, and, in contrast to the Teacher's withdrawal from others, to reach out in tangible expressions of compassion and love to those who are less fortunate than I. I am thankful the Teacher's Sacred Story is in the Bible. I am also thankful that it is not the only story.

A RIGHTEOUS MAN WHO DARES TO COMPLAIN

The other book in the Bible that might fall under the category of philosophy is the Book of Job. Thomas Carlyle called it "the greatest thing ever written with pen."[2] Job wrestles with the age-old dilemma of why bad things happen to good people. The perplexing problem of why innocent people suffer continues to be one of the greatest, if not the greatest, challenges to faith. Some writers have even called it the only problem worth discussing.[3]

The opening lines of the book repeatedly state that Job is a "blameless and righteous" man (Job 1:1; 1:22)[4]. Even God acknowledges to "the Satan" that Job is above reproach (Job 2:3). Quickly, however, Job's fortunes change, and without warning God's favor gives way to God's withdrawal and everything is taken away from Job—his livestock are stolen, his property is destroyed, his children are killed and finally Job is robbed of his health.

The calamities that befall Job are not due to his moral or ethical failures. Instead, God has made a wager with Satan that even if Job loses everything, he will still honor God. Why has God put Job's faith to the test? The answer is startling and may be one of the most troublesome passages in the Bible. God tells Satan, "You incited me against him to destroy him for no reason" (Job 2:3 NRSV). Everything that has happened to Job serves no great redemptive purpose, there is no divine plan in Job's misfortune. He has lost family and wealth—everything—for no reason! Seven sons, three daughters have been destroyed all because God wanted to play a game of chance with Satan.

The Old Testament scholar Samuel Balentine writes: "The occurrence of *hinnam* [the Hebrew word for "no reason"] in Job 2:3, far from being theologically benign, sets in motion an act that would elsewhere be associated with sin and therefore discouraged and condemned."[5] Balentine calls this phrase one of the "worry words" in the grammar of faith, making Job 2:3 one of the most disturbing passage in Scripture for those seeking to make sense of life with God.

When we turn to the commentaries for help there is little offered, as most writers ignore the phrase. The malignant words "*for no reason*" metastasize throughout the entire Bible and challenge the basis for faith in a benevolent Creator. "*For no reason*" cannot be summarily dismissed by any person who takes Scripture seriously. Balentine summarizes a comment made by Coleridge that the very existence of such a passage confirms that the Bible is an "utterly human production because God would never have written such a powerful argument against himself."[6] The theologian Carol Newsom creates additional discomfort by adding that Job's suffering can only be explained as "gratuitous destruction."[7] By any rational or moral standard the actions of God are inexcusable.

When we live life from one day to the next in the shadow, feelings that God has let us down or is indifferent to our circumstances block out any ray of spiritual light. Life with God turns cold and barren and lonely. It is not that we lose faith in God; we lose faith in a God who matters. What kind of a God is this who gambles with human life?

Anyone who has gone through a crisis of faith can identify with Job. Some years ago I was in a hospital room with a husband who had just lost his wife to cancer. The wife was a young and vivacious woman whose death was unexpected. The husband was furious with God. Standing by the bed of his dead wife, he shouted and cursed at God. At that moment I did not try to assuage his pain. I simply stood with him, with my arms around his shoulders as he denounced God, repeating the same words over and over again, "You bastard! You bastard!" While the words appear profane and may be offensive to some, they exposed the raw wounds of his soul.

The husband does not stand alone in hurling insults at God. The prophet Jeremiah joins the grieving husband and launches an even harsher verbal barrage when he accuses God of sexually assaulting him. He feels that he has been deceived and angrily denounces God: "O Lord, you have enticed me, and I was enticed; you have overpowered me, and you have prevailed" (Jer. 20:7 NRSV). The English translation, unfortunately, does not convey the pain-filled emotions of Jeremiah's heart. The word "enticed" has violent sexual connotations in Hebrew. The humiliated and rejected prophet literally accuses God of sexually molesting him. Specifically, Jeremiah condemns God, "I was a virgin and you raped me" (Jere. 20:7)[8]. Compared to the husband's profanity-laced tirade, Jeremiah's accusation rises to a new level of impertinence.

Unrelenting divine absence can crush the most resolute faith. The cold shoulder of God has a way of magnifying our pain and disappointment, rendering us spiritually numb. What words escape from our mouth are not thoughtful and considered, but simply the hard and bitter cries of rage. But, if prayer represents our innermost feelings, a window into our heart, then even vulgar words can be the heartfelt expression of faith in the ears of God.

There are times when there seems to be no rhyme or reason why life falls apart. Disappointment, anger, and even swearing at God may be the best we can do. After all, we have been created in the image of our Maker. We have been given the right to be completely honest with God about everything that we feel, even when those feelings express the bitter dregs of our soul. Job, in fact, does more than just complain—he puts God on trial for his actions.

PUTTING GOD ON TRIAL

Job does not know that his suffering is *"for no reason,"* that he is merely the bargaining chip in a divine bet. For the remainder of the book, he maintains his innocence and points his finger at God for being cruel, unfair or even intentionally out to get him. In the chapters that follow the introduction Job calls God to the witness stand and interrogates the Lord of the universe.

In chapters 9 and 10 Job confronts God in a kind of court of the imagination. In 10:1–2 Job's examination begins: "I loathe my very life, therefore I will give free rein to my complaint and speak out of the bitterness of my soul. I will say to God: Do not condemn me, but tell me what charge you have against me" (NIV). Job insists that God tell him what he has done to merit his inexplicable suffering. "Bring on your charges, bring on your witnesses," Job appears to be saying.

I would be remiss if I didn't mention Job's friends. There are three of them, with an additional intruder joining the conversation later in the book, and throughout the story these friends, I use the term loosely, criticize Job for his lack of contrition. The dialogues pivot back and forth between Job and these well-intentioned but misguided traditionalists. The friends do not waver from the accepted theological reason why people suffer: suffering is the result of sin. Proverbs 12:21 might have served as their key memory verse: "No harm befalls the righteous, but the wicked have their fill of trouble" (NIV).

Job, however, continues to hold his ground, refusing to concede that he has sinned. To add evidence in his case against God, Job claims in chapters 12–14 that God's justice is flawed and in 12:16 Job ridicules God as a deceiver of people. God creates nations, Job tells us, only to destroy them (Job 12:23), and ruins the lives of those who have been faithful (Job 12:19).

Job has every reason to believe that his vituperative rage will cost him his life, but that does not stop him from vehemently arguing with God. In desperation he cries out, "Why do I put myself in jeopardy and take my life in my hands? Though he slay me, yet will I hope in him" (Job 13:14–15 NIV). This passage as it is translated suggests that Job will remain faithful to God even if it cost him his life. It is a beautifully sentimental translation that has emboldened people of faith through the ages, but unfortunately, the passage may be incorrectly rendered.

In the Hebrew language the phrase commonly translated "I will hope" (Job 13:15) is "lô yāḥal." The word "lô" can also be pronounced as the negative "no" (lō'yāḥal), thus, "I have no hope," yet traditional English translations have made a theological judgement and chosen to interpret "lo" as the preposition "in," consequently the reading "I will hope in him."[9] So which translation preserves the original intent? Does Job cry in despair, "I have no hope" or does he confidently rejoice, "I will hope in him"? The ancient scribes suggest both translations are correct. The two possible translations may reflect the different stages of faith. How we interpret this passage leans heavily on whether we are enjoying the sublimity of God's presence or suffering through the dark shadow of God's absence.

When life comes crashing down around us, an either/or answer to this question seldom serves as a cathartic balm to our pain-riddled lives. Most often we hedge our bets by both trusting and doubting God's faithfulness. Perhaps the passage is purposely ambiguous to account for faith's double nature. Both belief and unbelief are components of a healthy faith and relate to each other as day does to night. In any life with God we experience both cycles over and over again.

The Book of Job is my favorite book in the Bible. I find in its pages an authentic expression of faith—a faith that is sensitive, alive, curious, angry, hurt, confused, beset by doubts. In other words, a real faith with all the emotions intrinsic to being a person of flesh and blood. Many in the faith community have been erroneously taught that it is heretical to confront God with questions challenging divine justice and fairness. Certainly, Job's friends believed that attacks on God's character were way off base. Bildad, one of the friends, speaks for many when he criticizes Job and lashes out, "How long will you say these things, and the words of your mouth be a great wind?" (Job 8:2 NRSV). Bildad ridicules Job and calls his words only empty and profane chatter. He, and all those who share his traditional theological reference point, feel obliged to defend the honor of God. Toward the end of the book another friend, Elihu, has heard enough of Job's tirade against God and tells Job that he is of little consequence in the scheme of the universe. Why doesn't Job just shut his mouth, admit his guilt and submit to God? (Job 37:14-24). Is passive acceptance of life's tragedies the prescribed model for people of faith?

Listen to God as he speaks out of a whirlwind in chapter 38:2 (NIV): "Who is this that darkens my counsel with words without knowledge?" Is God threatening the shivering Job, implying something like "How dare you challenge me? You have no idea who you are talking to!" Job's friends and the more traditional interpreters think so. God is finally putting Job in his place. At last, God has had enough of this complaining, impudent Job. For the next several chapters God gives Job a piece of God's mind and a lesson on how the world works. Job sees the error of his ways and is driven to his knees and repents in dust and ashes (Job 42:6). End of story, right?

While this traditional understanding may appear to tie all the loose ends and resolve Job's tension with God, Balentine wants us to pause before we close the book. He listens closely to the text, precisely parsing words, meanings and contexts. He observes that if God were simply trying to intimidate Job into silence, then why does God continue speaking after Job places his hand over his mouth? (Job 40:4-5). Could it be that God desires not to silence

Job but to encourage him to speak?

In Job 40:10 (NIV) God says to Job, "Then adorn yourself with glory and splendor, and clothe yourself in honor and majesty." Such words are used only to describe kings and God in the Old Testament. God, Balentine stresses, is not rebuking Job; God is honoring Job! Wow! Think of what Job has said to God, and now God, instead of condemning him, exalts him![10] And to rub salt into the wounds of Job's friends, friends who have insisted that Job must admit his sin and submit meekly, God reprimands them! God's rebuke pulls no punches. God speaks to Eliphaz: "I am angry with you and your two friends, because you have not spoken to me what is right, as my servant Job has" (Job 42:7 NIV). God is vindicating the Jobs of the world, the husband who cursed God, and all those who angrily scream to the heavens at the injustices and cruelties of our human existence. God has Job's back and the backs of all those who find themselves facing the inexplicable horrors of life.

JOB'S INSIGHTS INTO GOD

The haunting phrase that Job suffers "for no reason" is never explained. We are not, however, asked to passively accept life's unjust and tragic realities. When life falls apart apparently for no reason, Job reminds us that we have standing before God. We are privileged to voice our anger, complaints or any negative feelings without fear that we will incur God's wrath. God not only invites our pain-filled expressions, but, according to Job, they represent real faith.

Although the Book of Job resonates with people struggling through the darker periods of faith, it is not a completely pessimistic book. There are even some bold statements that project encouragement and hope. In spite of God's cavalier wager with Satan, the Book of Job emphasizes that human beings have value. God bets on and believes in the servant Job. In addition, God engages in conversation with Job, a rare phenomenon in Scripture.

Then, too, the phrase uttered by Job in the concluding chapter, "I despise myself, and repent in dust and ashes" has connotations that are missed by many English translations (Job 42:6 NIV). It appears on the surface that Job admits his guilt and falls before God in humble resignation, but perhaps we need to take a closer look.

The coupled words "dust and ashes" only occurs three times in Scripture. Once in Genesis 18:27, where Abraham bargains with God over the fate of Sodom and Gomorrah. He confesses to God that he is only dust and ashes. Is Abraham belittling himself before God? What is fascinating about this passage is that a few verses earlier some ancient versions read that God remained standing while Abraham speaks (Gen. 18:22). In later copies of the book the scribes changed the sentence because they thought it was unfit for God to stand before Abraham. After all, God does not stand before an inferior creature. But in the ancient wording that suggests that God remained standing before Abraham, the Bible is asserting that God places an inestimable worth on human beings—dust and ashes are the chosen materials of God's greatest creation. So precious are dust and ashes that the Lord of Creation stands in their presence.

In 30:19 Job appears to succumb to the traditional view that man is mere dust, of no eternal significance. His undeserved suffering and God's lack of response leaves the dejected Job with the conclusion that existence is more of a curse than a blessing, and in the scheme of things his life is inconsequential to God.

But all that changes after God speaks from the whirlwind (Job 38). Job has been granted an audience with God and has been allowed to protest the injustice of what has happened to him. God does not chastise Job but rather clothes him in honor and majesty. In response, Job changes his mind about his place in the world, and he recants or repents concerning his standing before God, for he now knows that he is not just dirt to God; on the contrary, dust and ashes represent the crown of God's creation. It is not a term of humiliation but one of grandeur and magnificence.[11]

Throughout Job's ordeal he had fallen into the traditional reasoning that human life was of little value to God. But now, in light of God's word, he changes his mind. Because God has not silenced him but given him an audience to lodge his grievances, he has come to realize that "dust and ashes," far from being a term of worthlessness, actually reaffirms that human beings have been created only a little lower than God and are the crown of creation. Made from the earth, we creatures of flesh and blood stand above all else as images of God's presence.

Then, too, Job grows to see that life with God is not a cosmic rabbit's foot. Living a life of virtue and honor and integrity does not spare us from the calamitous effects of life in the world. Bad things will happen to good people. They happen all the time. Innocent suffering is one of life's sordid truths. Job teaches that when our world collapses for no reason, we have the right to be bitter, to stand toe-to-toe with God and give God a piece of our mind and heart. Job's friends counseled him to humbly submit and confess his sin, but

Job reacted vigorously against their advice and for good reason—his suffering was undeserved. His loss of family, wealth and health occurred through no fault of his own, and he had every right to lash out at God. In chapter 42 God commends Job for his bold truth-telling and rebukes Job's friends for their false theological guidance.

A final lesson from Job tells us that God has a lot of explaining to do. Countless human beings suffer far more than they deserve. From our vantage point God appears rather inattentive and uncaring. What is clear, however, is that immense and inexplicable suffering destroys lives indiscriminately, whether righteous or unrighteous. The Bible provides little help in resolving this problem of innocent suffering. The theologian Kenneth Surin recognizes that the problem of evil defies explanation by writing, "Evil and suffering in their innermost depths are fundamentally mysterious."[12] If we choose to venture faith in God, we will live under this persistent shadow, and, if there are answers, they will not be forthcoming in this world.

We do not live in a fairy tale world. Life is cruel and unfair. Even though I am a person of faith, I frequently shake my head in frustration at the apparent indifference of God to much of the world's suffering. I am not alone in my discontent. By reading the Sacred Stories I have met other people who questioned God's reliability and faithfulness. They, too, were often disillusioned, and sometimes doubted how or even if God was attentive and caring. Some who journeyed through this darker region called for God to defend God's actions, and through their remarkable faith stories I have learned that I do not have to remain silent. When we find ourselves in the shadow for no apparent reason, we have a right to protest and express our feelings and be heard—a God-given right! For we dust and ashes are the crown of God's creation, and even the Lord of the universe stands in our presence!

CHAPTER 13

SURELY THIS IS GOD'S PRESENCE

It is not some meditative communion with God that I crave.
What one wants during extreme crisis is not connection with God,
but connection with people; not supernatural love, but human love.
No, that is not quite right. What one craves is supernatural love,
but one finds it only within human love.

- Christian Wiman

In the Bernese Oberland region of Switzerland there is a chain of spectacular mountain peaks, the most famous of which is the Eiger. It is sometimes called the White Spider because of the snowy spidery-like legs that mark the center of its north face. The granite peak rises a little more than 13,000 feet above sea level. Neighbors to the west of the Eiger are the Monch and Jungfrau, both of which have elevations hundreds of feet higher than the Eiger. But the magnificent face of the Eiger's north wall is what attracts tourists from all over the world. It is the most foreboding and perilous challenge for climbers in the Alps and was the last peak in Europe to be successfully conquered. Even today only highly experienced alpinists dare to risk the formidable north face.

Other than the vertical rock wall that ascends more than two miles into the sky, and the ice that continually melts only to freeze again at night and the constantly falling chunks of rock and ice, the ascent is hazardous because of the unpredictable weather patterns. As late as July snowstorms can blanket the mountain and jeopardize the lives of climbers. On the Mittellegi Ridge, east of the north face, a small hut has been constructed as a rest station for less seasoned climbers. The hut can also serve as an emergency shelter in case climbers get caught in an unexpected storm or an accident renders a climber disabled. The hut offers weary adventurers a respite from their strenuous trek.

I think the community of faith serves a similar purpose for people who have chosen to venture faith in God. I have found this faith community within the church. The church represents not a building of any describable shape, but an amorphous collection of people who have formed community by following the way of Jesus.

Communities of faith, because they are comprised of people, have tremendous transformative power to shine light into the darkness and, when defined by compassion, humility, and love, faith communities can incarnate the love of God through flesh-and-blood human beings. There is no greater transformative power than the touch of another human being.

Whenever we are touched by someone who genuinely cares, we feel more hopeful, as though a heavy burden has been lifted. Sometimes the touch can be physical—another person may hold our hand during a time of crisis or put an arm around our shoulder or speak a word of compassion or encouragement. Other times we experience a human touch through a timely phone call, text message or card received in the mail. We may feel warmth and tenderness when someone brings a meal to our family during a time of tragedy or illness. There are a variety of ways a community of faith can reach out to another human being, and, when done as an unselfish act of love, the possibility of God's presence becomes real.

In its finest hours the community of faith has been there for people needing shelter of one form or another. Sometimes the faith community provides refuge for people who no longer can put one foot in front of the other, who feel as though God has lost their address. At other times the community welcomes with joy the camaraderie of people celebrating their abundance of blessing. Authentic faith communities have room for all people regardless of where they are in their faith journey. The community, at first glance, may appear rather common. We are, after all, just people from all walks of life, and we are not differentiated from others outside the faith community by halos circling our heads. Yet, through this flawed group of flesh-and-blood people, the possibility of God's presence may be revealed and experienced.

The Bible teaches us that life with God cannot flourish apart from other human beings. While there may be times when we retreat from the world in order to think and pray, we can fulfill our spiritual purpose only by establishing I-Thou relationships. God's presence is most palpably experienced through community, and this is especially true for those mired in a land of "gloom and chaos, where light is as darkness" (Job 10:22 NRSV), when God seems remote or even non-existent. A.J. Gossip was right: "You people in the sunshine may believe the faith, but we in the shadow must believe it. We have nothing else."

To "believe the faith" implies community, for without other people faith becomes an exercise in self-worship. Throughout biblical history the faith community has steered individuals away from idolatrous acts of false worship. To believe the faith acknowledges that we need other human beings to lean on, to encourage us, to love us unconditionally, to help restrain our impulses, to rejoice and fellowship with, and to weep with. If we are honest with ourselves, it is not religious dogma that comforts us during trying times, but the touch of another human being. We find supernatural love through human compassion and understanding.

Only in community can we learn what it means to love one another, our highest moral challenge. Many of the Sacred Stories place love for others at the forefront of what it means to be created in the image of God. These stories teach that in loving the stranger, the unwanted, those who have been crushed by life, and all who suffer, not only does the presence of God radiate from our lives, but in the process we can experience life with God as well (1 John 4:12).

There have been occasions in my life when despair had a strangle hold on me, times when light seemed as darkness. I could not pinpoint any particular reason for my feelings of profound hopelessness. I only knew that God seemed not to care, to be even malevolent. I identified with the psalmists who often mourned that God had turned away or was irresponsible. That's exactly how I felt. I went about my work as best I could, but there was an emptiness and spiritual melancholy deep within. What kept me going, however, was the remarkable community of faith that encouraged me and stood by me. I would confide in a few of the leaders concerning my spiritual sluggishness and was overwhelmed by their love and support and prayers. Instead of reprimanding me or questioning my ministerial credentials to lead, these men and women affirmed me, and when I had little spiritual strength, I leaned on them and they kept me from faltering. An older deacon once shared with me while we sat on a riverbank fishing that he would be with me even if I felt God wasn't.

Jesus was not so fortunate with his friends. In his night of suffering in Gethsemane, he prayed to God to stay his execution, to allow him to live, but his plea was met with deafening silence (Mark 14:32–41). Now with his soul distressed, with anxiety over his impending death running at a feverish pitch, he needed more than ever the support of his chosen friends, the disciples, with whom he counted on most, but they could not keep watch with him. To be with someone in their suffering means to share their burden, to understand and to comfort. Surely, if God wasn't there *with* Jesus, his closest friends would be. But they weren't. He faced his trial utterly alone.

When we have been crushed by life's cruelties our only sense of God's presence may come through the weak and fallible lives of other human beings who are *with* us. The faith community can bring comfort and hope to those in the shadow by simply being present. When we are lonely and feel hopeless, when our lives are riddled with pain of one kind or another, a gift of inexpressible hope is given when someone cares enough to share our burden. The Spanish Philosopher Miguel de Unamuno understands the value of human presence when he writes: "The chiefest sanctity of a temple is that it is a place to which men go to weep in common."[1] Those who weep with us share our pain and may reveal the most tangible way that God's presence can be experienced among human beings.

Earlier, I wrote of my friend, Steve, and his battle with cancer. During this tragic ordeal that ended with his untimely death, Steve mourned the lack of God's presence. He desperately wanted some sense of assurance, some clue as to the outcome of his treatment but none came. Yet, even in God's silence, divine presence was not completely absent. He wrote in his blog:

> But what has been present is a timely e-mail, phone call, gift, card, text, or visit. People from literally all over the world have reached out. From Nicaragua to Birmingham, to Paducah, to Benton, to Asheville, to Memphis, to Charleston to Covington, to Cincinnati. And it goes on. I was totally oblivious that such a wide network of people would become connected to my situation. Surely this is God's presence.

"Surely this is God's presence." Through human acts of kindness and love my dear friend experienced the presence of God. Human touches became the gentle caresses of a divine love that were deeply personal. When our world is turned upside down, if we look for God to make some grand and spectacular entrance into our lives, we may be disappointed, but, if we are fortunate enough to find shelter and refuge with other human beings who reach out to us in compassion and love, we may very well discover a supernatural love.

In the story of the two disciples on their way to Emmaus after the crucifixion, Luke highlights the necessity of human community in experiencing divine presence. After seeing Jesus die the two disciples' faith had been shattered and their hopes darkened. As they spoke of the terrible events concerning Jesus' death, a stranger joined them as they walked. The two disciples did not recognize the unknown person as Jesus even when he explained the Scriptures to them. When they arrived at Emmaus, the two disciples invited the stranger to dine with them. At the table Jesus took bread, gave thanks and then broke it and gave the bread to the disciples, a clear allusion to the Lord's Supper, and their eyes were opened and they recognized him, then "he vanished from their sight" (Luke 24:31 NRSV).

The disciples became aware of divine presence after the breaking of bread with a stranger, an act of hospitality that unknowingly opened the possibility for an encounter with God. The breaking of bread with other human beings may uniquely describe what it means to be in community. Sitting at the table, sharing a meal with others, presupposes friendship, caring, love, intimacy and it is noticeably personal. People breaking bread in community create an aura not unlike a family gathering where they interact with each other in openness and affection. In this warm atmosphere the disciples' eyes were opened and they were able to look back on their journey from Jerusalem and realize that divine presence had been with them all along ("Were not our hearts burning within us?" (Luke 24:32 NRSV). Sometimes fellowship in community can awaken a sluggish spiritual memory and elicit a forgotten consciousness of God.

In community we are better able to fulfill our role as bearers of God's image to build bridges between people instead of erecting walls. Bridges open a path for understanding where faith communities can lead in the work of reconciliation between people (2 Cor. 5:17–20). The Apostle Paul calls these people who build bridges "ambassadors." The purpose of an ambassador is not to insist on conformity to a particular agenda or ideology, but rather to faithfully represent the one who has sent him. If Jesus is an incarnation of God's presence, as I believe he is, then by following his way of life, we fulfill our role as God's ambassadors.

As God's ambassadors, building I-Thou relationships become our great-est priority, our mission on earth. Broken and strained relationships with other human beings betray a misunderstanding of what it means to be in relationship with God. Micah 6:8 encapsulates the heart of the life of faith:

> *He has showed you, O man, what is good.*
> *So what does the Lord require of you?*
> *To act justly and to love community solidarity*
> *and to walk humbly with your God.*[2]

Neither justice nor love can be separated from what it means to be in community. The phrase "to love community solidarity" is translated "mer-cy" in some translations, yet the Hebrew word *hesed* extends beyond the word "mercy" to include a shared community's practice of love.[3] The phrase implies intimate social bonds. Jesus echoes this perspective when he teach-es that the two most important commandments are, first, to "love the Lord your God with all your heart and with all your soul and with all your mind." The second commandment is coupled with the first: "Love your neighbor as yourself" (Matt. 22:37–40 NRSV). These commandments represent the twin mountain peaks of both the Old and New Testaments. There is no higher standard.

C.S. Lewis writes in his children's story *The Last Battle*, the final book in the Chronicles of Narnia series, that even when our theology is off the mark, if our heart is in the right place, God honors the intent. A worshipper of a pagan god is surprised by Aslan's welcoming gesture and says to the Christ-figure, "But I said, Alas, Lord, I am no son of Thine but the servant of Tash [a pagan god]. He [Aslan] answered, Child, all the service thou has done to Tash, I account as service done to me."[4] Wherever faith communities practice love for God and neighbor, the work of reconciliation takes place, and when bridges of understanding and fellowship are built, God counts it as service rendered unto God.

Since people are fallible as are all theologies, no faith community is without flaws. When people suffer they may turn to the faith community and expect more than what the community can give. I realize that people in pain sometimes have little patience. There have been times in my ministry when the only comfort I could give was to sit with a grieving person and weep with him. There are limitations in caring for another, but what the faith commu-nity should always provide is understanding, encouragement, and hope.

There are practical ways that the faith community can incarnate divine presence for those in the shadow. The following examples are not exhaustive, of course, and serve only as a starting point. First, a faith community can hold its members accountable to live selflessly and compassionately. Second, a faith community can provide a safe environment for people to express their doubts and fears. Third, a faith community can practice acts of love. Fourth, a faith community can strive to be an inclusive family for all peoples. Briefly, I will outline how a faith community may become a people of understanding, encouragement and hope to those who feel shunned by the church or abandoned by God.

A COMMUNITY OF SELFLESSNESS AND COMPASSION

The cross is the unique symbol of the Christian faith. The crucified Jesus depicts an extraordinary picture of selflessness and compassion in contrast to a religion of mere comfort and consolation.[5] When I became a Christian during my teen years the cross represented for me a powerful sign of life over death. It functioned like a religious amulet worn around the neck to protect me from harm. Little did I understand the weighty significance of the cross.

Dietrich Bonhoeffer's book *The Cost of Discipleship* changed my understanding. Bonhoeffer, who was executed by the Nazis in 1945 only days before the war's end, continues to be one of the guides in my spiritual journey. Bonhoeffer realized the cross was not a good luck charm but an instrument that symbolized self-denial and death to destructive patterns of behavior and ambition. The measure of a faith community cannot be calculated by financial strength or numerical growth, but only by how faithfully it follows the way of Jesus, that is, the way of the cross. Bonhoeffer writes:

> *Self-denial is never just a series of isolated acts of mortification or asceticism. It is not suicide, for there is an element of self-will even in that. To deny oneself is to be aware only of Christ and no more of self, to see only him who goes before and no more the road which is too hard for us. Once more, all that self-denial can say is: "He leads the way, keep close to him."*[6]

The compassionate sacrifice of one's life in selfless service to another represents a human's highest calling. For a Western culture consumed with greed the cross signifies solidarity with the poor, the downtrodden, the broken, the misunderstood and forgotten of the world. The cross aligns people of faith with the alienated of this world. Obviously, those who choose to live the crucified life stumble and fall along the way, but an authentic faith community has its marching orders. Jesus plainly invites anyone who seeks God to "deny themselves and take up their cross and follow me" (Mark 8:34 NRSV).

If the faith community will follow the way of the cross, those who are alone, sick, and disenchanted with God will never be without support and compassion. Those fortunate enough to be enjoying God's presence are reminded to be a blessing to others. The cross reminds us that we have moral and ethical responsibilities far beyond ourselves, and are called to live sacrificially by standing with those who are forgotten, misunderstood and rejected by the world.

A COMMUNITY OF OPENNESS AND TRANSPARENCY

A faith community has many of the characteristics of a loving family. Home is a place where we can be ourselves without fear, where we can relax, express our views, and disagree with other loved ones without being exiled from the family.

My wife and I have two grown sons of whom we are proud. We taught them to be independent thinkers and we succeeded beyond our wildest dreams! Both men walk their own path, and their views regarding politics, science, philosophy, and religion often challenge our way of thinking. We are thankful they do not walk in lockstep with us, and we encourage them to evaluate information for themselves, and we respect and honor their ability to arrive at different conclusions than we do, and we trust they always feel comfortable challenging our ideas and beliefs. We think their independent mindset enhances our family. That's not to say that on occasion we don't get annoyed with our sons. We do. But we also know for there to be a healthy re-lationship, they must feel the freedom to think for themselves, even if their opinions do not align with ours.

A healthy faith community likewise creates an environment where people can express their views without feeling out of place. People yearn to feel at home when they enter into a community fellowship. It is more important that the community welcomes the questions and maverick ideas than try to conform everyone to a particular way of thought. In matters of religious faith any dogmatic embrace of only one perspective is the equivalent of having no perspective at all.

One Monday morning I received a call from a man who had attended our church the previous day and was upset over his treatment. He and his wife had visited a Bible study class where the virgin birth was discussed. After several minutes of conversation someone asked the guest what he believed. He replied that he did not think the virgin birth was a necessary Christian belief. There were several members in class who immediately reacted with visible anger and disgust. These few members inquired why he and his wife even bothered coming to church. To reject such a pivotal doctrine, in their opinion, was a denial of faith. Of course, met with that manner of gracious Texas hospitality, the couple made a hasty retreat to the parking lot where they climbed into their car and drove home.

I listened to the distressed caller for several minutes and tried to reassure him that not all people in the church were like the ones he and his wife had encountered. "Please return," I pleaded, "We have many wonderful people who would respect your opinion and welcome you." They did not.

I was grieved that he and his wife had found such an inhospitable environment in the church I served. I envision a faith community where it is safe to question the most hallowed belief, where people feel free to dissent, complain or even express frustration or anger with God. A faith community that does not attentively listen to those struggling with the God question loses the opportunity to build bridges of reconciliation. It is certainly not inappropriate to disagree with someone, but in doing so we should always respect the other person and show sensitivity and love. In the community of faith humility and doubt are virtues. The sensitive Catholic priest Henri Nouwen insightfully writes that boundaries of church life are sometimes drawn through fear, not love. And "fear," Nouwen adds, "never gives birth to love."[7]

A faith community provides an environment where people can feel safe, where they can be vulnerable and transparent—all traits of a family relationship. A family does not insist on conformity but recognizes contributions from all family members. In a family, members are unafraid to think differently or bring up uncomfortable issues. We can learn even from those with whom we disagree.

There are countless desperately lonely people who are searching for a faith community where they can be loved and cared for, where they can grow in their spiritual journey. Sometimes they have little understanding about theology and may not even care, but what they hunger for is acceptance and unconditional love. Jesus models for us a community that is similar to a family where people are received just as they are, without strings. Yes, the community may challenge our thinking, but we will never feel rejected or alone, and we will always feel welcomed.

A COMMUNITY WHERE ACTS OF LOVE ARE PRACTICED

I have a friend who grew up in the church but over the last several years has begun to question his early religious upbringing. For a time he and his family were part of a congregation I pastored, but he was transferred out of state and for a time we communicated mostly through e-mails and text messages.

He struggles with many of the traditional doctrines of the Christian faith and, consequently, had difficulty finding a new congregation. Finally, they settled on one, a little more conservative than he felt comfortable with, but the people were friendly and it was close to their home.

One Sunday his Bible study class called attention to a young widowed mother of several children who was having to move out of her house into an apartment because of financial issues. My friend inquired when the family was moving, and when informed, he suggested the class provide assistance, maybe care for the children or fix a meal or find a way to help with expenses. The idea fell on deaf ears. They were willing to pray for the unfortunate family, but to put forth physical effort, well, that thought never crossed their mind.

Prayer is certainly an important expression of faith, but if our prayers are divorced from practical acts of love, then we have failed to understand a major component of what it means to pray. A healthy faith community looks for down-to-earth ways to promote justice and compassion in its neighborhood and beyond, and through prayer our eyes are opened to a larger and needier world.

In the Old Testament the unwillingness to pursue acts of justice and righteousness brought divine judgement. Both justice and righteousness relate to the treatment of the poor and the less fortunate, and the terms have strong economic overtones. Often justice and righteousness in the modern faith community are perceived as adjudications of legal matters or personal traits of piety, but in Israel as well as the early church these spiritual disciplines encompassed benevolent treatment toward those on the margins. In addition, the term compassion in both testaments refers to empathy for those who suffer. According to the Sacred Stories, all three words, justice, righteousness, and compassion, are intrinsic to the character of God, and because these qualities are divine characteristics, they are to be practiced by those who seek life with God.

Theologian Gordon Kaufman writes that faith communities have a responsibility to act, to act morally and to act ethically.[8] Wherever a faith community exists one of the primary concerns is to practice acts of love. What are the needs of a particular area and how can the faith community help? Maybe free English classes for immigrants or maybe a free medical clinic for the poor or maybe low-cost daycare or even something as simple as a kind word for the person bagging our groceries at the super market. Some faith communities are building "tiny homes," small temporary dwellings where people can live when they have lost their places of residence for one reason or another. Practicing acts of love and kindness create an environment for I-Thou relationships to take hold, and wherever people are reaching out to others selflessly and compassionately, the presence of God is not far behind.

A COMMUNITY OF INCLUSIVENESS

When asked what the ugliest word was in the English language, poet Carl Sandberg allegedly said, "Exclusive." Many of the biblical witnesses would agree. The prophet Micah envisioned a day when "Many nations will come and say, 'Come, let us go up to the mountain of the Lord, to the house of the God of Jacob. He will teach us his ways, so that we may walk in his paths'" (Micah 4:2 NIV). Life with God begins by learning God's ways—ways that lead to a more human and humane world. God's intention was for Israel to be a blessing to all nations (Gen. 12:3) by doing "what is right and good in the Lord's sight" (Deut. 6:18). A case can be made that doing what is "right and good" begins by loving neighbor (Matt. 22:37-40).

Jesus hammered home this vision of inclusivity by announcing "Whoever does God's will is my brother" (Mark 3:35 NIV). The will of God, according to Jesus, is to feed the hungry, clothe the naked, visit the sick and the imprisoned, and welcome the stranger (Matt. 25:31-46). When God throws a party,

God extends hospitality to those who are considered outsiders—the poor, the crippled, the blind, and the lame (Luke 14: 13–24).

Fellowship with those who are different appears to be a mark of an authentic faith community throughout the Bible. God's reconciling love and concern for all people filters through virtually every page of Scripture. The God revealed in Jesus dined with tax collectors and prostitutes, Pharisees and fishermen, the rich and the poor. The Bible emphasizes that our neighbor is not simply a social equal or someone from a similar cultural background, but neighbor includes the outsider, the one who believes differently or even the one who was formerly perceived as an enemy.

Faith communities are diverse populations, and criteria for acceptance into these communities should not be based on narrow theological dogma but the desire to follow the ways of Jesus. Significant "wiggle room" allows each follower of the Jesus way, regardless of religious tradition, the freedom to think outside the box. A healthy faith community is not a bastion of theological orthodoxy, but a fellowship of ordinary people, people who long for God, who strive to build bridges of reconciliation between people of different religions and cultures.

A week after the resurrection of Jesus the disciples gathered together, presumably to discuss the strange happenings of the previous days. Only a week earlier the risen Jesus had appeared to them and changed their world forever. Thomas, who had not been with the other disciples the previous Sunday, was also present. What I find remarkable about this story, especially in the light of so much exclusivity within today's modern church, is that Thomas was with them.

Thomas was not a believer in the resurrection of Jesus, the core Christian belief, yet he was not excluded from their fellowship! The disciples had tried to convince Thomas that Jesus was alive, but he refused to accept their testimony. Unless he saw the risen Jesus for himself, he would not believe. Even though Thomas did not believe in the fundamental truth of the Christian faith, the disciples did not reject him from their community. Community overrode everything else. The affection, concern, and love for another human being was of greater significance at that point than theological correctness.

Authentic faith communities should not be in the business of excluding people. Faith communities should work tirelessly to bring people together in mutual respect and understanding. If we strive to be people of faith and rise above petty self-interests and seek reconciliation with all, a more human and humane world may slowly emerge. I have been convinced from reading

Scripture that through human acts of love the supernatural love of God may be personally experienced.

DESPERATE TIMES

Few things of importance have guarantees, and just because we involve ourselves in a faith community doesn't mean that all our problems will be solved. We can count on misunderstandings, hurt feelings, and vigorous disagreements with others, but in fellowship there is also the opportunity to grow as human beings, and, through the mystery of faith, experience God. In I-Thou relationships we not only come to know the other person, but we also come to know ourselves. Healthy faith communities move us toward fulfilling our purpose as bearers of God's image. In spite of our flaws, we can be symbols of hope whenever we strive to live in community with all others, and through a faith community we may discover the "personal" nearness of God.

Over fifty years ago Richard Rubenstein wrote that the utter hopelessness of the human situation desperately beckons for authentic religious communities.[10] Rubenstein, a Jew, tells of the terrible events of World War II and the effects it had on the Jewish community. After the war many Jews abandoned their faith. One of those Jews who had turned his back on God in the death camps was Elie Wiesel. After seeing the horrors of Auschwitz, Wiesel could no longer believe in the God of his childhood.

Yet, Wiesel could never completely give up on God. He continued to explore his religious feelings and later in life returned to faith, albeit not the faith of his childhood. Still, Wiesel recognized the value of faith communities and the hope these communities symbolized.

In Wiesel's book *The Gates of the Forest* the main character, Gregor, continually troubled by the aftershock of the war, converses with the Rebbe.[11] The war has ended but the memories have left emotional and physical scars that will forever mark Gregor and all those who survived the death camps. Gregor struggles with the God question and asks the Rebbe, "After what happened to us, how can you believe in God?"

The Rebbe faces Gregor and replies, "How can you not believe in God after what happened?"

If future holocausts are to be avoided, I believe life with God is the best hope. God did not murder six million Jews. That responsibility lay with those who worshipped a golden calf, religious people whose god only mirrored their worst impulses. In the final analysis much of the world's troubles we bring upon ourselves. Countless people suffer every day, not because material resources are scarce, but because many of us have forgotten that we were put here to be God's representatives on earth. Our worst human instincts such as greed, selfishness, religious bigotry, and fear pit us against each other as adversaries, whereas, if we recognized our common humanity as children created in the image of God, many of our problems could be resolved.

But not all of them. Unfortunately, there would still be tragedy and suffering, sometimes for no apparent reason. Children will be stricken with incurable illnesses, young adults will unexpectedly die and older people will be ravaged by disease and old age. We will continue to suffer more than we deserve. God, indeed, has a lot of explaining to do.

I have not given up on God, although my understanding of how God involves divine presence in my life and in the world has dramatically changed. If God is at work in our lives as I think God is, God's ways are subtle, indirect, and mysterious. God does not seem to care much for dramatic stage entrances. God works in quieter and less obvious ways. When I feel the crushing weight of unjust suffering, which often leads to doubt, anger, and spiritual disillusionment, I feel as though I am being sucked into an orbit of unending despair, but then there always seems to be someone who pulls me back—a conversation with a friend or a call from someone in my past, maybe a note from a former staff member or an invitation to share a meal—and through their human touch, full of grace, love, and understanding, I am reminded that I am not alone. There are people—common, ordinary people, flesh-and-blood people—who care about me, a community of faith who loves me and stands with me through the exhausting crucible of life.

Whether we choose to participate in a faith community is a personal decision. A life apart from a faith community does not exclude us from God's love and care, but it might exclude us from the love and care of others, and how can we possibly experience the presence of God without others? Then, too, a life separated from other people may result in the creation of a god who is only a mirror reflection of the self.

By forming community with other flawed human beings, especially through I-Thou relationships, by practicing acts of love, by listening to the Sacred Stories of faith, and by allowing people the privilege of voicing their pain and rage to God, we may find surprising places of hope that lighten the darkest day—places where belief and doubt, joy and sorrow are seamlessly woven together. This journey of faith will include uncertainty and risk, disappointment and heartache, but along the way our hearts will be warmed by the companionship of others, and we will never be alone. Surely this is the presence of God.

EPILOGUE

ANI MAAMIN

Every morning when you wake up, before you reaffirm your faith
in the majesty of a loving God, before you say *I believe* for another day,
read the *Daily News* with its record of the latest crimes and tragedies
of mankind and then see if you can honestly say it again.

- James Muilenburg

Do you remember the Christmas Eve story? I've never been able to put that night behind me. In many ways it was similar to the almost forty other Christmas Eve services I attended during my pastoral ministry, but that particular one lingers in my mind. I continue to think about the people whose eyes revealed anxiety, fear, and sadness. The young mother with breast cancer died a few months after the New Year. I stood by her bed as she left this world. Her small daughter cried softly in the adjoining room, confused and frightened. The widowed man who was going blind lost his sight. He now lives much of his life dependent on others. The father, who lost his wife as well as the mother of his two sons, struggles from one day to the next. The oldest of the sons, who was in the car when his mom was killed, fights chronic depression and has had a difficult journey. The scars of tragedy have carved deeply into their hearts, and they live with enduring grief.

These people represent only a fraction of those who were under my care during my years in the pastorate. A pastor sees a lot of suffering and heart-ache and absorbs a lot of pain from those who are hurting. In truth, anyone who sits with one who suffers shares a portion of that burden, and while the three friends of Job were misguided in their theology, I give them credit for at least being there with Job. To be present with those who suffer is a great act of love.

While some people quietly turn their backs on God when disaster crushes them, others continue with their faith community. On Christmas Eve we can find them in church and the following week they may appear again. Sunday after Sunday, month after month, people in the shadow join in fellowship and worship with their faith communities. Why? Why do broken and spiritu-ally wounded people continue to darken the doors of a church when they feel God has abandoned them or is indifferent to their pain?

The answer, of course, is complicated but maybe one explanation can be found in the community of faith. The one slice of hope these beleaguered people have is the connection they feel with other human beings. When your life falls apart, the faith community alone may be all that stands between you and despair. The faith community may fill the void left by an elusive and mysterious God, without which we might languish in a spiritual death spiral. God, indeed, may be absent from our life but in gathering with others, we will not feel so alone, and, in the presence of other human beings, the darkness we feel will be less frightening. True, life in the shadow may not yet be over, and maybe it will never end, but if we are embraced by a faith com-munity that practices acts of love, reminds us of the Sacred Stories, allows us to shake our fist in the face of God, and encourages us to develop I-Thou relationships, we may very well find hope.

Life with God is not some magical or supernatural emotional high that encompasses us. We live life with God when we live in harmony and peace with each other. In this world God has chosen to reveal divine presence through the flesh and blood of human beings, through the love and concern and compassion we experience in I-Thou relationships. We may self-con-sciously attend a worship service with people of faith, shoulder to shoulder with those whose unconditional love has kept us from cratering, and think, "I am not alone. I am not giving up. There are people here who care about me. Surely this is God's presence."

Those of us who struggle with faith in an attentive and personal God dot the church rolls. We hang on by our fingernails to religious belief. The writer Christian Wiman grasps the volatility of life with God when he notes that one of his friends wakes up a Christian but goes to bed an atheist.[1] There are many of us like Wiman's friend. Earlier the Teacher reminded us that there is much in life that seems absurd, and to risk faith in a loving and caring God can stretch our integrity to the breaking point, but in I-Thou relationships God may not seem so very far away.

The God question, for me, remains elusive. I have learned to live in the shadow, with its limited light, but at least it is not completely dark. In the shadow there is still hope, and where there is hope, there is the possibility of meaningful life. I identify with the man in the Gospel of Mark: "I believe; help my unbelief." How I would love to visit with that man, who also lived in the shadow. I think he would say to me that he never would have made it without the love and friendship of other human beings. Whatever comfort and consolation there is in matters of faith, we find it primarily through human relationships. Heaven is other people—all kinds of people, red, yellow, black and white. People who worship differently, think differently or speak languages strange to us can all contribute to a fuller, more meaningful and hopeful life—a life with God.

Over the years I have spoken with a number of people who desperately yearn for some sense of God's presence, yet feel only loneliness, emptiness or even rejection. Some of these people are burdened with chronic illnesses that dampen or even obliterate any sense of God; others simply have analytical minds that naturally question many of the traditional dogmas of faith. Still others have life experiences that make faith in a loving and caring God too great a barrier to cross.

People barely managing to hang on to faith, or on occasion those who have given in to despair, have often questioned me, "Pastor, do you think there is a place for me in the faith community? I'm not sure I believe in anything." The fact that people would even ask such a question reveals how far the faith community has strayed from understanding its purpose in the world. The community of faith should be the one place where everyone feels welcomed. After all, where else can people experience the goodness and love of God? Outside a faith community there is no place else to go where broken and hurting people are unconditionally accepted and loved, where they can experience the presence of God.

Regardless of whether we journey in the bright light of God's presence or in the dismal shadow, in reality we all walk shoulder to shoulder in varied shades of darkness. The cloud stands between all of us and God. In this world only a thin ridge separates belief from unbelief, hope from hopelessness. The most confident believer may be only an unexpected tragedy away from shaking her fists at God and cursing the deafness of heaven or completely abandoning faith.

Medieval paintings characteristically picture biblical figures like Joseph and Mary or the disciples with aureoles. The light encircling the head was meant to indicate that the person was holy, a saint. In truth, all halos are tarnished. All of us, even the biblical men and women, have feet of clay, as the Bible makes clear time and again. In the world as it is, "rejoice in the Lord" is only a heartbeat away from "My God, my God, why have you forsaken me?" Ironically, it seems that a healthy faith is a tad paradoxical.

What Elie Wiesel saw and experienced in the death camps defies imagination. His naïve understanding of God was shaken, and his faith was forever robbed of its innocence. How could a loving God allow such unimaginable horrors to take place?

A Hebrew song that was periodically sung in the death camp was Ani Maamin, "I believe." The refrain, "I believe in the coming messiah, and though he tarry, yet will I wait for him" inspired the young Elie not to lose hope in the face of incomprehensible circumstances. The grotesque suffering and senseless death the teen witnessed day after day challenged his faith to the core.

One night several Talmudic scholars came to Elie and invited him to a trial. Elie had never been to a trial and thought it would be an interesting experience.

When he arrived at the "trial" he was shocked to learn that these devout Jewish scholars were putting God in the dock. God would face accusations of dereliction of divine duties and criminal neglect.

Witnesses were called and came forward presenting testimony against God. They told of seeing the most terrible crimes—babies, children, mothers, old people murdered while the Master of the Universe stood idly by. After all the testimony had been presented, a verdict was announced: "Guilty." God had been found guilty of crimes against humanity.

After the verdict was announced, all the people, including the scholars, went back inside and observed their evening prayers. Ani Maamin, I believe! Side by side belief and doubt, joy and sorrow, merged together to describe what it means to live a life of faith, a faith that knows both light and shadow.

Why did these people who had suffered so much go back inside and say their evening prayers? Had they not found God guilty of neglect? Why should they even bother with God? Many of us have asked the same question.

I think it was because they still believed that God was in some mysterious way present with them, maybe not directly, maybe not in the way they would have liked, but just the same, God, in some wonderful and tangible way, was so very near. Even in their unimaginable suffering, they could sense divine presence.

They felt God's touch when another anguished soul reached out to them in tenderness and love. They heard God's voice when someone whispered a word of encouragement. They saw God's presence when someone found food scraps and in spite of his own hunger, shared them with others. They overheard God weeping through the sorrowful prayers of fellow sufferers mourning the dead. The people went back to their prayers because they sensed sacred presence everywhere, all around them—it took only eyes of faith to see divine presence in the dust and ashes of fellow human beings, creatures so utterly magnificent that even God stands in their presence.

Created a little lower than the Almighty, adorned with glory and splendor, honor and majesty, we creatures of flesh and blood are privileged to raise our voices in protest, to rage at the heavens, to feel despair, and to scream and curse at the evils and injustices of our world. And yet, though all may seem loss and God far away, we will still sing, Ani Maamin! I believe! For in every faith community there are human beings, frail and fallible creatures, who bring near the mysterious and awesome presence of God.

ENDNOTES

Christmas Eve
[1] Wiesel, *Night*, 25.
[2] Wiesel, *Night*, 32.
[3] Wiesel, *Night*, 34.

Chapter One
[1] Gossip, *When Life Tumbles In*. Gossip delivered this sermon shortly after the death of his wife.

Chapter Three
[1] I am indebted to Richard Beck for helping me to see the parallels between the "sick souls" in the works of the psychologist William James and the "wintry faith" of theologian Martin Marty (See *The Authenticity of Faith*, 99–147. There are certainly more than two seasons of faith, just as there are more than two personality types. Marty's model, however, provides a useful tool in helping us to see a general personality pattern among people of faith. People, as a rule, lean toward either a more summery disposition or a wintry one.
[2] See Brueggemann, *Theology of the Old Testament*.
[3] Brueggemann, *Theology*, 318.
[4] Cited in Beck, *Authenticity*, 122.
[5] Buechner, *Telling the Truth*, 55.
[6] Beck, in fact, reports that "generally speaking, Christian believers (and believers from other faiths) use faith to repress, hide, avoid, or deny the existential realities of human existence." (*Authenticity*, 146). Beck's statement may offend us, but his extensive research makes for a compelling case.

Chapter Four
[1] Becker, *The Denial of Death*, 50–51.
[2] Becker, *The Denial of Death*, 55.
[3] Eliot, *Four Quartets*.
[4] Brown, *Augustine of Hippo*, 110.
[5] Irwin, *God is a Question*.
[6] Irwin, *God is a Question*.

Chapter Five

[1] Author's Translation

[2] Lewis, *The Lion, the Witch and the Wardrobe*, 86.

[3] More will be said about the importance of community in the later chapters.

[4] Soelle, *Suffering*, 107.

Chapter Six

[1] Taylor, *Sources of the Self*, 217.

[2] The relationship God established with Israel and the church, often called covenants, has been frequently misunderstood as providing special privilege for the "chosen ones." Whenever Israel interpreted her "chosenness" as giving her special status before God, the prophets were quick to condemn (Amos 3:2). The covenants are not contracts that reward their recipients with exclusive claims on God. Rather, covenants are agreements of obligation whereby the chosen ones commit to being messengers of truth and bearers of love to all peoples. (See Newbigin, *The Gospel in a Pluralistic Society*, 80–88. The Hebrew word for "to choose" (bhr) implies responsibility. Israel and the church are singled out to "enflesh" God's unfolding intention for a more human and humane world, not because God loves them more, but because they are to serve as instruments for implementing God's plan for all peoples. In much of the biblical story God's love is not limited to any particular group but stretches to all corners of humanity and embraces "all the families of the earth" (Ps. 117; Amos 9:7; Rom. 11:32).

[3] Yancey, *Reaching for the Invisible God*, 99–112.

[4] Yancey, *Reaching for the Invisible God*, 102.

[5] See Willard, *Hearing God*.

[6] Willard, *Hearing God*, 67.

[7] Willard, *Hearing God*, 69.

[8] Yancey, *Reaching for the Invisible God*, 106. See John 5:39 for Jesus' understanding of the place of Scripture as a means of grace.

[9] Willard, Hearing God, 71.

[10] Robert Jones' extensive research into white supremacy among American evangelicals attributes the concept of a personal relationship with Jesus as a contributing factor to racial intolerance. As bizarre as this may initially sound, when people believe that they have a favored status with God, then their worst impulses can be easily justified. See Jones, *White Too Long*, 95–106.

[11] Heschel, *Man's Search for God*, 10.

[12] Boring, *The Gospel of Matthew*, 204.

[13] Author's Translation

[14] In Matthew 1:21 God's Son is called Emmanuel, "God with us," emphasizing the community. Both testaments stress the importance of knowing God through community. The Apostle Paul's letters were addressed to communities. The preposition "with" also has significant connotations. God is not just "for" us, but God is "with" us, signifying a much greater involvement. How we experience God's personal nature in our lives is the focus of this book.

Chapter Seven

[1] Author's Translation

[2] While Martin Buber's comment may be offensive to modern ears, his thought is worth pondering given the nature of today's casual approach to God: "He who begins with the love of God without having previously experienced the fear of God, loves an idol which he himself has made, a god whom it is easy enough to love. He does not love the real God who is, to begin with, dreadful and incomprehensible." See *The Eclipse of God*, 36–37.

[3] Von Rad, *Genesis*, 208.

[4] Terrien, *The Elusive Presence*, 83.

[5] Kierkegaard, *Fear and Trembling*, 10–11.

[6] Armstrong, *The Case for God*, 39.

[7] See Noth's *Exodus* in The Old Testament Library, 257–258 and Rylaarsdam, *Exodus*, 1070.

[8] See *The Cloud of Unknowing*, Ed. by Emilie Griffin, 11.

[9] Terrien, *The Elusive Presence*, 28–29.

Chapter Eight

[1] Tillich, *Systematic Theology*, 244.

[2] Tillich, *Systematic Theology*, 245.

[3] Human beings created in the image of God have the capacity for heart-warming good or unspeakable evil. During the Nuremberg War Crimes Tribunal S. Szmaglewska, a Polish guard in Auschwitz, tells how near the end of the war children were thrown into the crematorium alive. He stated that the children's screams could be heard throughout the camp (Cited in Surin, *Theology and the Problem of Evil*, 14.) Such evil perpetrated by human beings forces me to wonder if God doesn't regret the creation of our human species.

4 Buber, *I and Thou*, 85.

5 Buber, *I and Thou*, 57. See also Buber's Eclipse of God, 13–24.

6 MacMurray, *Persons in Relation*, 61.

7 Buber, *I and Thou*, 164.

8 Buber, *I and Thou*, 62.

Chapter Nine

1 Scriptural passages in both testaments emphasize that our vertical relationship with God is dependent on the horizontal relationships we have with each other. See Lev. 19:18; Micah 6:8; Matt. 22:36–40; Mark 12:30–31; Luke 10:25-37; 1 John 4:7–21.

2 Kaufman, *In Face of Mystery*, 322–333. See also Exod. 33:20–23; Job 9:11; 23:8–9; John 1:18; 1 John 4:12.

3 Both Gnostics and Montanists taught that they could have direct and unmediated experiences with God. The early church councils condemned these beliefs as heresies. See Manschreck, *A History of Christianity in the World.*

4 Wiman, *My Bright Abyss*, 72.

5 See "Eckhart, *The God Beyond God*, 1–19.

6 De Unamuno, *Tragic Sense of Life*, 188–89.

7 Peretz, "If Not Higher," 23.

Chapter Ten

1 Levenson, *Sinai and Zion*, 38.

2 Craddock shared this story at a Pastor's Conference at Candler Seminary in May of 1991. Momaday's early life's experience can be found in *The Names A Memoir* and *The Way to Rainy Mountain.*

Chapter Eleven

1 Claypool, *Tracks of a Fellow Struggler*, 72.

2 Claypool, *Tracks*, 70.

3 Beck, *Authenticity*, 129. Beck, a Christian psychologist, has spent years researching why people turn to religion. He emphasizes that many believers choose faith in God as a means to buffer them from life's great fears—sickness, loss of a loved one, death, etc. Beck also points out, however, that not all believers gravitate toward religion as an escape from these existential threats.

4 Crenshaw, "The Human Dilemma," 235–258.

5 Crenshaw, "The Human Dilemma," 238–244.

[6] Cited in Soelle, *Suffering*, 114.

[7] Cited in Marty, *A Cry of Absence*, 12.

[8] Psalms 90 and 39 are also bleak prayers to God that appear rather gloomy overall. The value of psalms like these is that they reflect how we in the shadow at times have felt about God. Before we relegate these laments as outliers to faith, we should first remember that they are prayers—petitions to God that express authentic feelings of reverent resignation. Nevertheless the prayers are addressed to God.

[9] Balentine, *The Hidden God*, 122. Here Balentine disagrees with the views of Old Testament scholars, Claus Westermann and Walter Brueggemann, who see the psalms of lament as preparatory to praise.

[10] Marty, *A Cry of Absence*, 87.

[11] Balentine, *The Hidden God*, 124.

Chapter Twelve

[1] Towner, Ecclesiastes, 302.

[2] Balentine, "Job," 3. I am indebted to Balentine's theological insights. His extraordinary commentary has contributed significantly to my understanding of Job.

[3] Balentine, "Job," 4.

[4] Author's Translation

[5] Balentine, "Job," 60.

[6] Balentine, "Job," 60.

[7] Newsom, "Job," 354.

[8] Author's Translation

[9] Balentine, "Job," 211–213.

[10] Balentine, "Job," 625–678.

[11] Balentine, "Job," 692–699.

[12] Surin, *Theology and the Problem of Evil*, 52–53.

Chapter Thirteen

[1] De Unamuno, *The Tragic Sense of Life*, 17.

[4] Author's Translation

[3] Wolff, *Micah the Prophet*, 109.

[4] Lewis, *The Last Battle*, 164. The Jewish scholar Abraham Heschel quotes from an ancient rabbinic commentary (Midrash) that if an unlearned Jew reads from Holy Scripture and mispronounces a phrase saying we-ayabta (and thou shall hate) instead of the correct reading we-ahabta (and thou shall love), in divine mercy God says: 'His

error is beloved to me.' God sees within a person's heart and not merely the outward form of service. See Heschel, *Man's Quest for God*, 17.

[5] Life with God most certainly will include comfort and consolation, but real faith should also include transformation. Transformation requires discipline, selflessness and perseverance, which defines the way of the cross. See Wilber, *One Taste*, for the distinction he makes between a translational faith and a transformational faith.

[6] Bonhoeffer, *The Cost of Discipleship*, 97.

[7] Nouwen, *Lifesigns*, 18.

[8] Kaufman, *In Face of Mystery*, 194–206.

[9] Author's Translation

[10] Rubenstein, *After Auschwitz*, 119.

[11] Wiesel, *The Gates of the Forest*, 194.

Epilogue

[1] Wiman, *My Bright Abyss*, 27.

EPIGRAPHS

Christmas Eve: Molly McCully Brown, *Prayer for the Wretched Among Us.*

Chapter One: James Crenshaw, *Traditions and Theology in the Old Testament*, p. 258.

Chapter Two: Roger Lundin, *Emily Dickinson and the Art of Belief*, p. 3.

Chapter Three: Samuel Balentine, *The Hidden God*, p. 173.

Chapter Four: William Irwin, *God Is a Question, Not an Answer*, N.Y. Times, March 26, 2016.

Chapter Five: Psalm 71:14(NRSV).

Chapter Six: Blaise Pascal, *Pensees* 585.

Chapter Seven: Isaiah 45:15 (NIV).

Chapter Eight: Martin Buber, *I and Thou*, p. 57.

Chapter Nine: Abraham Joshua Heschel, *God in Search of Man*, p. 35.

Chapter Ten: Barbara Brown Taylor, *When God Is Silent*, p. 114.

Chapter Eleven: Luther, Cited in Dietrich Bonhoeffer, *Life Together*, p. 9.

Chapter Twelve: Samuel Balentine, Job, *Smyth & Helwys Commentary*, p. 96.

Chapter Thirteen: Christian Wiman, *My Bright Abyss*, p. 163.

Epilogue: Cited in Now & Then, Frederick Buechner, p. 16.

BIBLIOGRAPHY OF SOURCES

Armstrong, Karen. *The Case for God*, Alfred A. Knopf: New York, 2009.

Augustine. *Confessions*, ed. Douglas L. Anderson, Broadman: Nashville, 1979.

Balentine, Samuel. *The Hidden God*, Oxford University Press, 1983.

———— Job, *Smyth & Helwys Bible Commentary*, Smyth & Helwys: Macon, Georgia, 2006.

Beck, Richard. *The Authenticity of Faith*, Abilene Christian University Press: Abilene, Texas, 2012.

Becker, Ernest. *The Denial of Death*, Free Press Paperbacks, Simon & Schuster: New York, 1997.

Bonhoeffer, Dietrich. Life Together, Harper & Row: New York, 1954.

————*The Cost of Discipleship*, Macmillan: New York, 1974.

Boring, Eugene, M. The Gospel of Matthew in *The New Interpreter's Bible*, Vol. VIII, Ed. by Leander E. Keck, Abingdon: Nashville, 1995.

Brown, Molly McCully. *The Virginia State Colony for Epileptics and Feebleminded*, Persea Books, 2017.

Brown, Peter. *Augustine of Hippo*, University of California Press, 2013.

Brueggemann, Walter, The Book of Exodus, in *The New Interpreter's Bible*, Vol. 1, Ed. Leander Keck, Abingdon: Nashville, 1994.

———— *Theology of the Old Testament*, Fortress: Minneapolis, 1997.

Buber, Martin. *Eclipse of God*, Humanity Books: Amherst, New York, 1988.

———— *I and Thou*, Charles Scribner's Sons: New York, 1970.

Buechner, Frederick. Now & Then, Harper & Row: San Francisco, 1983.

———— *Telling the Truth*, Harper & Row, San Francisco, 1977

Claypool, John. *Tracks of a Fellow Struggler*, Word Books, Waco, Texas, 1974.

Crenshaw, James. *Traditions and Theology in the Old Testament*, ed. Douglas A. Knight, Fortress, 1977.

De Unamuno, Miguel. *Tragic Sense of Life*, Dover: New York, 1954.

Eliot, T.S.. *Four Quartets*, Independently published, 2019.

Fretheim, Terrence E. The Book of Genesis, in *The New Interpreter's Bible*, Vol. 1, Ed. Leander Keck, Abingdon: Nashville, 1994.

Griffin, Emilie, ed. *The Cloud of Unknowing*, HarperSanFrancisco: 1981.

Heschel, Abraham J. *Man's Search for God*, Charles Scribner's Sons: New York, 1954.

———— *God in Search of Man*, Farrar, Straus and Giroux: New York., 1976.

Irwin, William. *God is a Question, Not an Answer*, N.Y. Times, 2016.

Jones, Robert. *White Too Long*, Simon & Schuster: New York, 2020.

Kaufman, Gordon. *In Face of Mystery*, Harvard University Press: Cambridge, Massachusetts, 1993.

Kierkegaard, Soren. *Fear and Trembling*, Princeton University Press: Princeton, New Jersey, 1983.

Levenson, Jon. *Sinai and Zion: An Entry Into the Jewish Bible*, Harper Collins, 1984.

Lewis, Clive Staples. *The Last Battle*, The Chronicles of Narnia, Macmillan: New York, 1970.

———— *The Lion, the Witch and the Wardrobe*, Macmillan Publishing Company: New York, 1970.

———— *The Problem of Pain*, Macmillan Publishing Company: New York, 1962.

Lundin, Roger. *Emily Dickinson and the Art of Belief*, Eerdmans: Grand Rapids, 2004.

MacMurray, John. *Persons in Relation*, Humanity Books: New York, 1999.

Manschreck, Clyde. *A History of Christianity in the World*, Prentice-Hall: Englewood Cliffs, New Jersey, 1974.

Martin, Marty. *A Cry of Absence: Reflections for the Winter of the Heart*, Harper & Row: San Francisco, 1983.

McCann, Clinton J. Jr. The Book of Psalms, in *The New Interpreter's Bible*, Vol. IV, Ed. Leander Keck, Abingdon: Nashville, 1996.

McGinn, Bernard. "The God beyond God: Theology and Mysticism in the thought of Meister Eckhart," *Journal of Religion*, Vol. 61, No. 1 Jan. 1981.

Momaday, Scott. *The Way to Rainy Mountain*, The University of New Mexico Press, 1969.

Newsom, Carol. The Book of Job, in *The New Interpreter's Bible*, Abingdon: Nashville, 1996.

Newbigin, Lesslie. *The Gospel in a Pluralist Society*, Eerdmans: Grand Rapids, Michigan, 1989.

Noth, Martin. Exodus, in *The Old Testament Library*, Westminster: Philadelphia, 1962.

Nouwen, Henri. *Lifesigns*, Doubleday: New York, 1986.

Panko, Stephen. Martin Buber, *Makers of the Modern Theological Mind*, Word: Waco, Texas, 1976.

Pascal, Blaise. *Pensees*, Digital Edition by Gianluca Ruffini, 2017.

Peck, Scott. *The Road Less Traveled*, Touchstone: New York, 2003.

Rubenstein, Richard. *After Auschwitz*, Macmillan: New York, 1966.

Rylaarsdam, Coert J. Exodus, in *The Interpreter's Bible*, Vol.1, Ed. George Arthur Buttrick, New York: Abingdon: Nashville, 1952.

Simpson, Cuthbert A. Genesis, in *The Interpreter's Bible*, Vol. 1, Ed. George Arthur Buttrick, New York: Abingdon: Nashville, 1952.

Soelle, Dorothee. *Suffering*, Fortress: Philadelphia, 1975,

Surrin, Kenneth. *Theology and the Problem of Evil*, Wipf and Stock: Eugene, Oregon, 2004.

Taylor, Barbara Brown. When God is Silent, Cowley Publications: New York, 1997.

Taylor, Charles. *Sources of the Self*, Harvard University Press: Cambridge, Massachusetts, 1989.

Terrien, Samuel. *The Elusive Presence*, Harper & Row: San Francisco, 1978.

Tillich, Paul. *Systematic Theology*, Three Volumes in One, The University of Chicago Press, 1967.

Towner, W. Sibley. The Book of Ecclesiastes, *The New Interpreter's Bible*, Abingdon: Nashville, 1997.

Trueblood, Elton, *Philosophy of Religion*, Baker: Grand Rapids, Michigan, 1957.

Weber, Ken. *One Taste: Reflections on Integral Spirituality*, Shambhala: Boston, 2000.

Weiser, Artur. The Psalms in *The Old Testament Library*, Trans. by Herbert Hartwell, Westminster: Philadelphia, 1962.

Wiesel, Elie. *The Gates of the Forest*, Schocken Books: New York, 1966.

———— Night, Bantam: New York, 1982.

Willard, Dallas. *Hearing God: Developing a Conversational Relationship with God*, Intervarsity: Downers Grove, Illinois, 2012.

Wiman, Christian. *My Bright Abyss*, Farrar, Straus and Giroux, 2013.

Wolff, Hans Walter. *Micah the Prophet*, Fortress: Philadelphia, 1981.

Yancey, Philip. *Reaching for the Invisible God*, Zondervan: Grand Rapids, Michigan, 2000.